Big Dreams, Bigger Excuses

The Book On Overcoming
The Reasons That Hold You Back From
Pursuing Your Dreams

Dan Wischnewski

Big Dreams, Bigger Excuses

Copyright © 2017 by Dan Wischnewski
All rights reserved

Neither this book nor any part may be reproduced or transmitted in any form or by any means, electronic or mechanical, including photocopying, microfilming, and recording, or by any information storage or retrieval system, without prior permission in writing from the author, except for the quotation of passages by a reviewer in print or through electronic mass media.

ISBN: 978-1-988215-11-2

Publishing Partners:

One Thousand Trees
www.onethousandtrees.com

Valen Vergara Ventures Corp.
www.valenvergara.com

Contents

Dedication	v
Foreword	vii
About This Book	ix
My Story	1
Chapter 1: Family, Friends, But Most Of All Strangers Own Me	35
Chapter 2: But Everyone In My Life Lives This Way!	39
Chapter 3: Why Don't You Shut Your Mouth? My Attitude Is Fine	43
Chapter 4: What's The Rush? I Have Plenty Of Time	47
Chapter 5: I Don't Know How! Do It For Me!	49
Chapter 6: I'm WAAAy Too Old Or WAAAy Too Young	51
Chapter 7: I Have No Bucks, No Connections, And No Help	53

Chapter 8:
My Mind Is Open To Change, As Long As I Don't Have
To Do Anything Different   55

Chapter 9:
Success And Failure Are Both Scary, So It's Best To Avoid Them 57

Chapter 10:
What's Your Vice? The Unspoken Excuse   59

Chapter 11:
My Past Sucks And The World Owes Me   61

Chapter 12:
I Am Always Tired, And I Can't See My Feet   63

Chapter 13:
I Have No Free Time! I Do Have Commitments To Facebook,
Twitter, Instagram And Netflix You Know!!   65

Congratulations!   93

*This book is dedicated to Alex Wischnewski.
What day does Daddy love you?
Every day!*

Foreword

The book, *Big Dream, Bigger Excuses*, could not possibly make its debut in a timelier period. These days humanity is experiencing more trials and tribulations of the mind than ever before. Most especially for the significant reason that a world in the wake of conflict is increasingly in dire need of mindset readjustment. Dan Wischnewski's authentic approach to tackling tough subjects is nothing short of astounding.

It is rather refreshing that the author makes it clear, right from the outset, that this literary journey is centered on overcoming the fears that hold people back from success. His reasoning then becomes apparent as he unpacks his own experiences dealing with troubling circumstances. The fact that he rose above it all is a feat in itself!

Dan demonstrates that anyone can accomplish whatever he or she believes in. Successful people have vision. To be a visionary means to be a dreamer. Some turn their dreams into reality while others let the dream die inside. Dan encourages people to mold, shape and create a physical representation of the dream they hold in their mind's eye.

Personally, I feel impressed by the author's raw and uncensored display of coming back against all odds. Truly inspirational! I am quite confident that after reading this book, if you are going through some difficult moments, you will resonate with Dan's writing and know you hold the power to stage a comeback! Moreover, this book challenges the conventional understanding of mental therapy and speaks directly to experiential healing.

Dan Wischnewski

In conclusion, I would like to express my sincere thankfulness to the author for taking the time to battle hardships and hold on, in and through turbulence! You are making life good for others!

Valen Vergara
Founding Director of The Worldwide Expedition for
Peace and Truth Project Inc.

About This Book

When reading this book please maintain an open mind to all the possibilities, and at the same time enjoy a sense of humor along with it. Learning new things and making change is so much easier when you have a smile on your face.

Like myself, most people can get easily offended (dramatically so) when they are directly confronted. Most are extremely quick to defend their positions. The word excuse is usually a hot button for most, because it implies there is something wrong with the person, that they are lazy, weak or even dishonest. The fact is, excuses are a deeply embedded self-defense mechanism. Excuses are used by most to protect them from a deeper meaning. I find the more someone defends inaction by using a multitude of excuses in a passionate way, the more that person feels the need to fulfill that which they say is impossible to do. The message within is simple to understand and yet hard to follow. To change everything, to become the person you truly wish to be and to live the life you have always dreamed, the very first step that opens the door to these possibilities is to be conscious of the voices in your head, and what you are allowing as truth. It starts with a simple decision to be consistently aware of your thoughts, and to see them for what they are. It is very easy to take the voices in as gospel and fact. When you begin to question what is holding you back and when you look at the "reasons" that are holding you back, under the microscope long enough, they will fall apart.

All excuses are an illusion created by the mind, manufactured by the primary culprit which is fear. Once that fear is identified for what it is, its power begins to lessen. In time fear will weaken until it no longer has a hold over you. This takes discipline, commitment and daily work, but becomes easier to do each day. At first, you will get an overwhelming feeling, when you realize the countless amounts of excuses that have run rampant in your mind, and what you have allowed your mind to create for so long. This can be a challenge to come to terms with as you realize that the excuses that were fabricated to protect you, in fact, were and are robbing you of your very destiny. After time and work the excuses weaken out and will be less in frequency. They will disappear and will only surface under dire circumstances, and even then will be destroyed by an aware, keen and perceptive mind. In time the excuses that have held you back for so long, and that had so much power over your mind, will be seen as laughable, and will be stripped of any power or relevance. The excuse voice will be that of a whiney child that desperately wants attention for all the wrong reasons. One that is told gently but firmly to go to sleep.

Imagine what your life could be like if you saw past the reasons you couldn't and focused on the reasons you should.

I once heard someone agree with person X, who had every excuse in the book for not following their dreams. They listened until person X presented their case with everything they had to offer as "proof" that chasing their dream was impossible. In the end the person spoke to person X in a tone that was understanding and non-confrontational, "What if it were possible?" Just pretend it is possible, just for a minute. What you would do first? It amazed me how that person's eyes went dark for a moment. They went back in the excuse void of their mind, then they lit up as they let it go for that brief moment. You could see the shift and rise in their energy level when they thought of what their first step would be. It was a huge load off their shoulders. After a brief period, the person went back to their old way of thinking of what they had accepted and hidden behind for so long. But it was a start! It was a first step to understanding what can happen with awareness and a shift in thought.

Big Dreams, Bigger Excuses

You can expect three takeaways from this book, which will drastically change your life if you chose to implement them.

- You will have a heightened awareness of the thoughts coming in and out of your mind.
- You will develop a security system, a mental shield against the disempowering thoughts.
- You will have a wide variety of methods and rituals that will aid you on your journey towards achieving your goal and living a life both inspired and at peace.

A portion of the book proceeds will be given to the United Way.

If you are interested in partnering with Dan in a Business Opportunity, please email bigdreamsbiggerexcuses@gmail.com.

My Story

You may ask why I am qualified to write a book on excuses and how to overcome them. I believe my story will answer that question. It is not my full biography but more of a quick overview of my life. I have only included some of the significant events that brought me to where I am today. You will then have a better understanding as to why I felt so compelled to write this book. I will do the best I can with the timelines, but there are times in my life that are pretty foggy.

I was born in 1973 in Winnipeg Manitoba. I was very lucky in the parents department; my parents are amazing. They are the most loving and supportive people out there. I have two older brothers that took great pleasure in beating me up when we were kids, but admittedly I brought a great deal of it down on myself with my big mouth. We are a close-knit family that includes a large extended family.

As early as preschool I can remember always feeling anxious and scared. My teacher at the time was harsh with most of the kids, and devastatingly cruel to me. She would call me names and made me feel like I was stupid. Still today, it's a very painful, vivid memory for me. She was so wicked that all the parents banded together to have her removed from the school. She was an older woman who was way past her retirement years, and borderline senile. Back in that day teachers could get away with things that would never be tolerated today. I can remember getting smacked in the head, having my hair pulled, and pushed around often. The physical treatment I endured was unpleasant, but the way she made me cry in front of all the other kids was what did the real damage. I believe that set the stage for my feelings towards school. You are supposed to trust a person in authority. When they tell you something, you believe it. I had learning issues and when I was told I was stupid, I believed I was stupid.

In elementary school I remember being the class clown because it was my way of coping and hiding the fact that I was having such a hard time learning. I didn't want the other kids to make fun of me so I figured If I could get them to laugh or even intimidate them they wouldn't notice my learning disability. I had actually become a bizarre combination of comedian/ bully. If you didn't laugh at my jokes, I would punch you in the face. A charming method of making friends, but temporarily effective nonetheless. Boy, did I struggle through my elementary days! I was consistently late with my homework, but I had the most creative reasons for why that was. I always had a particular person or extreme situation to blame as I pleaded my case to my parents at report card time. The truth was I hated having to do the work required. The work always took me so much longer than everyone else. It wasn't fair. This was the genesis of *the world owes me* thought pattern I adopted. Poor me! I was offered extra help from my parents and teachers, but I refused every attempt. I made it through because I became a master manipulator; somewhere along the line I acquired an unfortunate talent of having everyone do the work for me. There was always someone that I could befriend or threaten to take on my responsibilities.

I was a very headstrong kid who did not take direction well from anyone in authority. I spent many hours in the detention room, but of course it was never my fault. I was unjustly imprisoned by a corrupt school system that preyed upon the innocent. Even this early on in my life, I had a sense of emptiness, sadness, and lack of direction. I knew that there was something wrong with me; everyone else seemed so happy.

I did find a purpose in the latter part of elementary school. I joined a hockey league, and that became my life's focus. All the other kids involved had been playing hockey long before I started. I was by far the worst player on the team to start out. This was a blessing in disguise. For the first time in my life, I had a burning desire to excel at something. I remember thinking, "Laugh now because it's a matter of time before I am skating circles around you and butt-ending you with my stick." I am still not sure if my desire was to become a great athlete or just to get back at everyone who laughed at my ankle-bending methods of skating. I would practice every day, every second! Whenever I had the freedom, I would practice. I became a pretty decent hockey player. I didn't care if I had friends that showed up at the rink because nothing was going to hold me back! I preferred to be on my own anyway. I didn't want to have to count on anyone, because whenever I did I was let down and disappointed. So it was me myself and I passing the puck amongst ourselves.

I continued to play hockey in junior high. I tried out for one of the high caliber teams – the Triple-A. I had always played with the community club teams in the past. In the community club league, I was a standout player and I was the one that everyone noticed. I received all the attention. At least that is what I thought. I was meant for so much more than this substandard rec league. I went all in and I trained as I had never trained before. I went through the rigorous tryouts and made it all the way through to the final cuts. I sat in the dressing room and thought *is this happening?* After all that hard work my dream was about to come true! This realization triggered something deep within me. It was too much and I couldn't handle it. I couldn't handle the pressure and the expectations if I was to make the Triple-A team.

My inner voice said to me "Even if you make the team you will never keep up with everyone else; it's only a matter of time before you are exposed for what you truly are." The voice continued by reminding me that I had failed at everything else in my life and this would sadly be no different. It was best to just give up now. It would only hurt me more when I failed later. The last tryout, I put very little effort in. I had already given up!

I was instantly recognized as a weak link and cut from the team. I was devastated and relieved at the same time. I chose the coward's way out, and this has haunted me for my entire life. I went back to playing community club hockey and my skill level went down and down. My burning desire had been extinguished and the love of the sport was gone.

It was at this time that I realized I was always sad and anxious. I could be surrounded by groups of friends, but I still felt alone. I tried to do things that had brought me happiness in the past, but felt nothing at all. I didn't understand why I felt the way I did, but I certainly wasn't going to bring it up with anyone! I already felt like an outsider, different from everyone else. Back then depression and anxiety disorders were not openly discussed without condemnation. I figured if I just held on, things would get better.

I went on a quest, in search of something that would bring me lasting happiness. My new focus was relationships. I had always had a girlfriend from a very young age, but at that time hockey was my priority. Now that hockey was behind me, I jumped right into the dating scene. I was not what you would call a shy guy. I met a girl and I dated her for quite some time. With her I was honest, affectionate and giving. She was giving as well, but unfortunately to many other guys besides myself. The realization that my love was not reciprocated destroyed what little self-esteem I had left. I was humiliated because everyone but me knew of her infidelities. The lesson I learned was to trust no one, and treat your girlfriends badly because it's only a matter of time before they do it to you. I learned that the more I ignored a girl the more she wanted to date me. I could be rude and disrespectful and they would pursue me. The Bad Boy persona was adopted and became my way of life. I wouldn't let any of the girls get too close to me because I feared they would see through the act and leave me hanging. When I started to have genuine feelings for whatever girl I was dating, I would promptly do something outrageous so the relationship would end with my ego intact.

By some miracle, I managed to get through middle school with a passing grade, and started my high school career. I went to a high school that was preppie in stature. This school was very cliquey and clothing-oriented. Fitting in was a big deal, and not an easy task. I knew right out of the gate this was not the place for me. I stuck around because I had the opportunity to play for the hockey team. I had zero desire to play hockey, but I felt compelled as it was a connection to the party scene I craved. I made it my mission in life to get on this team. I trained harder than ever and I made it! The team was comprised of mostly seniors, so it was a huge deal that I was to be one of the few freshmen that made it. I used to love going to the parties to drink with the older kids. It gave me the opportunity to party and meet older girls. I did very little training once I received the coveted high school hockey jacket, and spent more time thinking of the next party rather than the next game. This attitude showed in my performance, so I spent the majority of my glory days riding the bench. It was very telling that whenever something became high pressure, where I would have to maintain a certain skill level or a certain amount of work, I would just give up.

The idea that I was in a high school to learn something or pass a course was ludicrous to me. I had all the time in the world to do the work later, so I was going to have fun right now, or at least find a reprieve from the emptiness that plagued me. I found myself hanging out with "bad kids" at the school. I spent more time at the smoking doors than I did in the classroom. These kids were fun! I starting drinking more, and started using dope. I started off with only a few tokes off a joint but, as you party people out there know full well, when you're drunk and you take a hit off a joint as a rookie, you are destined for barfsville. I was a frequent visitor to the bathroom until I was able to build up a tolerance; however, smoking pot didn't bring me the joy and euphoria I was promised. It didn't make me howl with laughter or have any spiritual awakenings. It made me dizzy, lazy, hungry and tired. Since that wasn't working for me the only responsible thing to do, in my mind, was to start taking mushrooms and dropping acid. These drugs did the job. The shrooms brought me a hilarious sense of freedom. They brought me closer to the people that shared the same journey. I felt a real connection with my fellow stoners. It sounds silly, but a great trust is required when going on a trip with someone. It was one of the first times I felt like I fit in with a group of people. Imagine the attraction to no longer looking in from the outside. I felt a part of something, and that felt good. As for the acid, this was not such a great experience. The majority of times that I dropped acid I committed some type of crime, got in a fight or did something crazy. During my last experience with acid, I tried to jump from a train bridge to a light post. I was unsuccessful. If I had fallen a foot to the right I would have been impaled on a street sign pole; if I had dropped a foot to the left, I would have broken my back on the concrete. I landed on a small patch of grass without any injury whatsoever. This was the first of many near-death experiences to come.

My life now revolved around drinking, using, and picking fights, and women. The principal at "preppie high" made me aware that I was no longer welcome at his learning establishment. They had had enough of me. I never showed up for class, I distracted other students, I started a lot of trouble, and they wanted to get rid of me. I was okay with going; I just wished they had brought this to my attention earlier. I had just recently acquired a new Ralph Lauren garment I was looking forward to modeling for my fellow classmates.

Off I went to a new high school. This particular high school was considered the rough school. This is where I went from being the preppie guy in the more affluent area, to a school full of people with long hair, tight jeans and leather jackets. I found myself quite at home with my fellow heathens. I started hanging out with a bunch of different groups. We were nonstop drinking and dope. It was kind of like Woodstock, only with a lot more punching. We brought forth a lot of excitement, danger, and a lot of trouble. Every once in a while we even made special guest appearances in the classroom.

I was still struggling with my undiagnosed depression and anxiety disorder. My alcohol and drug consumption was in my mind recreational, so life was tolerable until one fated night.

I went to a party with my girlfriend at the time, along with one of my closest friends. A guy in attendance made advances towards my girlfriend, so naturally an argument ensued. The confrontation sizzled out, and with my guard down I began to consume more beverages. My friend, my girlfriend and I decided to leave, so we jumped in the car and took off. As we drove down the street, two guys in a car cut us off and jumped out of their vehicle. It was the troublemaker from the party, with one of his buddies. I was not into this, and something didn't feel right. I had been in many fights, but my gut told me to steer clear of this one. By the time I tried to voice my concerns, my friend had already exited the vehicle and started exchanging blows. I stood by the car and watched it happen. I didn't want to get involved. The choice of being a spectator was taken from me when the troublemaker from the party joined in on my friend. In my books, there is nothing lower than double-teaming someone. It's the brother code; when your buddy is in trouble you have to step in whether you like it or not. I threw a very sloppy, slow and predictable haymaker of a punch. That's all I remember. The troublemaker easily avoided my strike and drilled me in the temple. Lights out for me! I went down hard. I was told that the guy kicked me over and over again while I was unconscious. In the ribs, my head and my face. When it was over, my friend and my girlfriend dragged me into the car and drove off. I remember my girlfriend screaming my name and my friend asking "Is he okay? Is he okay?" They took me to my parents' place. My poor parents had to see their son vomiting, screaming in pain. I refused any attempts to take me to the hospital, despite all their efforts. My ribs were broken, my nose and eyes were black, and my whole body was swollen.

This event scarred me for life. In one night I lost everything about who I thought I was. I was humiliated that not only did I lose a fight but was beaten almost to death. I immediately went into cover-up mode.

I used every excuse in the book to save face. I told anyone that would listen that I was too drunk, I slipped on ice and he sucker-punched me. None of this was true. I lost because I lost. I am a firm believer in karma. I received exactly what I had deserved.

I felt sorry for myself at the time, never thinking of all the people that I had hurt in my life. It took me months to physically recover. It took years to emotionally recover. I believe that I may have had PTSD. Going forward, I was constantly paranoid about going anywhere for fear that a fight might break out. I was very selective about where I went, so I stayed home most of the time. My fear eventually turned into anger, which then turned into rage. I wanted to get revenge but the opportunity never presented itself, nor did I pursue it. In the back of my mind I always asked myself the question, "What if I lost again to the same guy?"

Rage and fear are a toxic combination. So any chance that I got to get into a fight, I would take it because I wanted to prove myself, to myself and everyone else.

It took me five years to complete high school when it was only supposed to take three. I suspect the teachers took mercy on themselves and me because I managed to graduate with a solid 51% average. I did not even consider college or university because that was where the smart people went. I didn't feel I was smart enough to find the location of a higher learning facility, never mind attending one.
My next step, and only option as I saw it, was to enter the service industry. I am what you call an outgoing introvert. I can be loud, funny and entertaining when I must, but the real me prefers the majority of his time quiet and being alone. I harnessed my acting skills into working in the outgoing and loud industry. I started off as a busboy and climbed the ranks. I made an attempt at bartending, but it took a lot of work to learn how to make the drinks, so I promptly dropped that idea. I did, however, take to being a waiter. All I had to do was be funny, write down food orders and deliver the goods. Easy peasy and

right up my alley. I used to brag about how much money I made, and mocked the people that went to postsecondary school. I was quite short-sighted, and instant gratification was always my way of doing things. As a waiter I was also able to work at night, party after my shift with my fellow servers, and sleep all day long. That was my life pattern for many years. I would drift from groups of friends to different groups of friends, depending on the restaurant I was working at.

I never kept friends for that long because I was in party mode and a lot of my friends had actual plans for their life. I would get rid of the friends that would outgrow how heavily I partied, and I would naturally gravitate to others that would drink and use the way I did. Throughout this period I was pretty wild, and I would do anything for excitement, making life fun and impressing people.

I never really had any real trouble when it came to the police. Well, kind of. There is one instance in that period that I can remember. My friend and I were speeding down one of the main drags in Winnipeg while we were both wasted. The police turned on the lights and sirens and started chasing us. My friend, who was driving, was just as crazy if not crazier than I, and decided that we were going to outrun them. He hammered down, driving at mach speed, weaving in and out amongst cars. After we thought we had enough of a lead, he turned down a side street and eventually into a back alley. Thinking we were home free, we parked in a driveway and started belly laughing at how smart we were and how dumb the cops were. That was right up until the police silently pulled up behind us, lit up the lights and turned on the siren. I later told my friend that I spilled beer down the front of my pants, but I suspect he knew different. The police made us get out of our car. Being the smart ass I was, I of course asked what took them so long. There were not any cameras in the cop cars back then. The cops did not appreciate my sense of humor, so they gave us a few smarten-up shots to the body, but nothing major. Looking back, I clearly got what I deserved. They gave us a break and they didn't arrest us or bring us in. Just a couple of $99 fines for the open liquor.

After a stern lecture and a few more smacks, they left. There was a slight hesitation in their departure as they watched us flip them the bird. We were either unaware or didn't care that they had full use of their rear view mirror. We were left bruised but laughing. Falling on the ground laughing. We went into the back seat where we had our dope hidden, and the beer was waiting in a special compartment in the trunk. We stayed right there drinking and getting high. Of course, we had to tell all our friends what we had done so we would look like big men. That was the first brush with the law where things could have been severe. All I learned was that I could get away with this kind of behavior, made me bolder and more arrogant.

I jumped from restaurant to restaurant as a server. I usually would have to leave on the fly because whatever waitress I was dating would find out I was also dating her friend, sister, and in one case the mother. I was not what you would call a classy guy. I finally came across a restaurant that I called home for years. The waitresses there had more patience and a sense of humor towards my dating antics. I was living a life based on distractions and sadness. No matter what I tried, be it booze, dope or women, I still felt empty and alone.

It was at this time I started experimenting with hard drugs. I went from experimenting to addiction instantaneously. My life revolved around using cocaine. When I rolled up the bill for the first time, I felt like I was in a movie. When the drug hit my system, I remember yelling "Holy Shit! I feel incredible!" My confidence soared; I felt stronger, and at ease within myself. All my sadness, worries, guilt and fear disappeared. I was able to speak to people like never before. I discussed things that had been on mind for years, without any inhibitions. To put it mildly, I thought I had found the answer to all my problems. The only downside was that the feeling went away in a very short period. My new quest was to chase the dragon.

I loved where I was working because the majority of people there shared the same fascination with our preferred drug. When you spend time with individuals with the same vice, it becomes an acceptable way of life. It is not out of the ordinary for those involved. I continued living the way I always had, by partying all night and sleeping all day, but now party all night usually meant party till 8 in the morning or even later. Then I would sleep a few hours and go back to work again. Something called the coke blues set in within this brief period that I was using. When coming down from coke, there is intense sadness as well as paranoia. I already suffered from depression, so when I came down from the high, I was at a level of sadness that I had never experienced before. It was the first time I thought *Is this a life worth living?* I was never suicidal per se, but the urge to give up was always hovering somewhere in my mind. I was always broke, but now I was going into debt with the wrong people. I became a parasite. I would hang out with anyone that had dope, whether I liked them or not. I had no self-respect and lowered myself in many ways to acquire the drug. I was the definition of selfishness, and one hell of a con man. I was incapable of caring about anyone but myself, and getting my next high. It got to the point where I was always letting my family down, and all my "normal" friends wanted nothing to do with me. They saw the train wreck that I was becoming. With my debts mounting, I decided the best thing I could do was take a geographical cure, so I jumped on a plane with a hockey bag of clothes and moved to Vancouver.

A word of advice to anyone who is running away to get clean: running away never works, and Vancouver is not a wise choice. The drug scene in Van is insane. I spent a year living in Van as a professional bum. I moved into a house with about ten other people. I wasn't even invited. I was accepted in because my big brothers were living there at the time. I slept on the floor for the first three or four months that I was there. I did not work at all. My depression had taken over, and I wasn't able to function. I spent most of my time on welfare. I was collecting checks, and spent most of my days sleeping, reading, or smoking pot sitting on park benches. The only positive thing I gained from living there was I started reading books on self-help and spirituality. Little did I know what a role these books would play in my future!

My brothers moved forward with their lives while I stayed stuck. I'm glad they escaped the black hole that I had become. I never had any money, and I didn't have any connections, so I did get some clean time but it wasn't by choice. When I could get the hard drugs, I would jump on it. I lived with some great friends that took care of me. When I look back on it now, it was like I was their child. Even though they were partying (only with drinking and not using drugs) they maintained jobs, cars, etc. I had nothing. Whenever we moved from place to place they were stuck with me, and I would just go wherever they went. We did have fun at times, because our house was always the party house. I was able to distract myself with the women that came in and out of my life. I was still so lost and unhappy. I knew life had to change, but I didn't know how to change it. It was actually on the one-year anniversary that I had moved out there, that I called my parents and told them that I wanted to come home. My parents, being the loving people that they are, sent me a plane ticket. I decided that I would start a new life once I got back to Winnipeg. No more dope or partying. I decided it was time to make something of myself.

I started back at the same restaurant that I used to work at, only one week after I came home. I was certainly a glutton for punishment. I started using more than I ever had before. Now I was becoming sick. I had numerous trips to the hospital and I was scared my heart was going to explode out of my chest. My weight began to fluctuate to extremes. I wasn't able to eat solid food for days after a bender, and I started losing weight. I had always been very vain when it came to my body, which is not only ironic but was a lifesaver at times. I insisted on maintaining a certain amount of muscularity, so the only way I would go off of the dope was so I could eat and work out to get back to the look I desired.

No matter how low I went, I still cared what people thought of my appearance, but I didn't care much of what they thought of me. This certainly was a testimony to my personal depth.

As fate would have it, I started a relationship with a girl that despised cocaine. I cared about her, but I cared more for the dope. So it was a constant cat and mouse game when it came to me using. This girl and I decided we wanted a better life, so we moved to Calgary. She wanted adventure and I wanted to get away from all the trouble I had gotten myself into yet again in Winnipeg. This time, I thought, it was sure to work.

A short while after we were settled in Calgary, we both became gainfully employed as servers in two separate restaurants. I wanted to stay clean and live a better life, but in a few short months, the girl I was living with had enough of me. I was unable to use when I was with her, so I became a miserable and angry person. Everything that came out of my mouth was a complaint of some kind. I was very moody and rubbed most people the wrong way.

The moment I became single and acquired a place to live, things got crazy. I felt a sense of freedom that I had never felt before. I realized that I could do anything I wanted, without any repercussions, at least as I saw it. I had no girlfriend to keep me in line, and my family was in Winnipeg, so I didn't have to worry about hiding my addiction. I was determined to control my drug and alcohol use, but I was equally determined to live large. I made friends with people I was working with at the restaurant. These were good people and for the most part were not in the drug scene. They were people that were working to earn money for university so they would be able to find good-paying long-term professions.

No one there knew my history, so I had a clean slate. I worked my shifts and made it to work on time even after a bender. I did, however, start planning my benders on nights that I didn't have to work the next day so I could go much harder.

I went to underground bars and seedy night clubs because I knew that was where I would make the best dope connections. I went through a complete transformation as to the way I looked. I was working out hard in between benders, and I was putting on muscle mass. I shaved my head and grew a goatee so I would look and be able to take on the tough guy role. I hooked up with a group of people that were involved in the drug trade, and I gained their trust. This took some time, but I didn't care; I was given all the dope I wanted during the prove myself stage. This was another one of those it feels like I'm in a movie moments. It was surreal, exciting, dangerous and fun.

My role eventually became the enforcer. I was big and looked mean. I was a very talented actor because I wasn't a tough guy anymore, if I ever really was. I had not been in a fight in a long time. My recollections of violence were that getting hit hurt, so I wanted to avoid it as best I could. I would puff up and put on a convincing show, hoping that everyone would buy it. I spent the majority of my free time in this club, hanging with this group. The bar was my new home, and I loved it there. Within this club, there was an area upstairs where my group would hang out. This area was off limits to any outsiders. People would trudge up the stairs with the hope of scoring. I would be at the top, looking down as the gatekeeper. I had the power to allow safe passage or turn them away. I felt a real rush having power over people in that manner. If I gave the nod, they were sold dope by one of the fellow members and then sent on their way. I was getting in real deep into this lifestyle. I loved the attention, I loved the money, but it was getting dangerous.

There was one particular incident where a fella walked up the stairs, and I recognized him from television. He was someone that had starred in several TV commercials. His life had fallen apart because of the sickness. He went from being on TV with a bright future to losing everything. I was disgusted by what he was now, if only I knew what was to come for me. This former actor had gone into Safeway and stolen some steaks. His intent was to trade the steaks for cocaine. I had no interest in such a ridiculous transaction, so I bid him farewell. He was hurting bad and had the itch, so he became belligerent. I was very high at the time and would not allow others to see someone speak to me in such a manner. I had to take action or I would lose respect and standing within the group. After a brief struggle, I threw him off the railing of the stairs onto the ground below. It was a long enough drop that he was able to flail his arms once before crashing down onto the cement floor. I thought I killed him. He wasn't moving! The group had the area cleared out of any witnesses and made sure that if anyone saw what had happened they knew what the repercussions would be if they spoke out. The actor was picked up like a bag of garbage and brought outside. I was more concerned about what could happen to me since I thought I ended his life. When the actor was outside, he regained consciousness. He had sustained no serious injuries. He asked for his steaks back and went off into the night. I had heard he was back at the club the next day trying to barter with a toaster oven. It was a huge turning point in my life. I could have killed someone and lost my freedom. This is what I needed to finally realize the situation I was in. It was at that point that I started distancing myself from that group. The group was not like what you see in the news. They weren't powerful or ominous. It was just a group of guys that sold dope and hung out together. They could care less that I no longer wanted to be a part of the scene. They knew that there would be a next sucker to get involved and take my place. I gave up, as I saw it in my mind, the "rock star" lifestyle. No more free dope, no more money; the higher roller life was gone forever. Many of my fellow addicts had been disappearing in the last little while. They were all dying! I found out some were murdered, some committed suicide, and some overdosed. It was better to leave that scene before I wound up like one of them.

I still see the actor falling in my dreams. It haunts me to this day. I know in my heart that I will never hurt another human being again for the rest of my life.

I still carried on with my drug use, but it was impossible to earn the amount of money I needed for the amount of drugs I was accustomed to ingesting. I was always making shady deals to bring in extra income. The years of chemical abuse finally caught up with me. It now took a full week to get a semblance of my health back after a bender. I was having chest pains on a regular basis, and I lost a substantial amount of weight. I could no longer stomach food; anytime I ate I would throw up. Due to my fading health, I could no longer maintain any job. I was so sick and depressed that I would lie in bed for days. There were times that I didn't even have the strength to get up and use the bathroom. Movies make drug addiction look glamorous; this is far from accurate. In that period I was living with another girl. She did everything she could to help me. She had seen glimpses of the person I could be, so she was determined to help me get my life back. It was a mission that was doomed from the get go. I had an endless amount of excuses as to why I couldn't get better. I blamed every person, place or thing for my sickness. "It wasn't my fault, and I just need more time to get clean."

Every person has their limits, and she had hers. I came home after a long party night to find all my possessions sitting in her back yard. I was sick, broke, hopeless, and now alone. I hadn't showered or eaten in days. My nose was still bleeding, as it often did, and my heart palpations were significant. I lay down on the ground and decided to die. My history in these types of moments had always been to beg for another chance at life. Instead, I asked death to take me and end my suffering. I have no idea how long I was lying on that cold ground, but I do know that even death didn't want me. I picked myself up and gathered whatever belongings I could. I loaded up the car that was at the house, that was kind of mine at the time, and I drove off. I started driving with nowhere to go. During my time in Calgary, I had managed to let down, rip off and disgust anyone I came into contact with. I had lowered myself to such levels that I didn't care what I did to others or what they did to me. All that mattered was getting high so I could have a moment of peace before hell took over again. I had no choice but to live in my car. This former high roller was now begging for change on the street.

I looked very sick, and I was an excellent con man, so anyone who would listen would give me decent bucks. I wish I could say that I was humiliated by this, but I was too far gone to care. At night when I slept in my car, I was in a constant state of panic. I was paranoid to the core. I was convinced someone was going to smash the window and stab me in my sleep. I eventually had to give back the car to the rightful owner or face the consequences. Now I was officially homeless. I had all that I owned in my backpack. I would beg for money during the day and get high as often as I could. I would befriend any other person I could who used, and who could give me shelter for the night. Otherwise, I slept in the parks.

One day while I was walking around thinking of what to do next, I looked down at my feet. My runners were dirty and ripped, and you could see my toes sticking out. At that instant I had an Aha moment. I thought, *if only I had shiny shoes to wear.* I was meant for more than this. Somewhere in my fog-addled mind the message that I was to become so much more than I was became clear. I felt something I can't explain come over me and, for a brief moment, I felt at peace.

I called my parents, who were completely unaware of what I had become, and asked them if I could come home. They immediately said yes and sent me yet another plane ticket. My parents' act of love saved my life.

When I got off that plane, I was probably around 140lbs. I was all skeleton, no flesh, and I looked like I was dying. The second my parents saw me they knew that something was seriously wrong. I will never forget the look in their eyes. The fear and worry for their youngest son. I finally came clean and told them what I was doing and how I was living my life. I censored a great deal of it. I vowed never to put them through this again. I felt something I hadn't felt in a long time, a conscience, and concern for someone other than myself.

I immediately called a 12-step recovery group and went to my very first meeting. The room was filled with the most supportive people that you could ever imagine. I was surrounded by individuals that had been through similar experiences. It felt good to feel like I fit in somewhere. I started the program and began getting my health back. I quit using for close to a year. I used to go to meetings every single day; they became my life. I lucked out with a great job in the fitness industry as well. I was making real progress.

I always thought if I had my life back I would be happy. This was not the case. All I felt was emptiness, sadness, and most dangerously boredom. I realized the 12-step programs were not something I believed in, so I stopped going to the meetings. I felt like they were wasting my time. I had a job, my own place, and a car. I was doing the best I had ever done. I would never go back to what I was. I adopted a false sense of confidence. That was when the whispers started. My mind had blocked out all the pain and suffering I had endured in Calgary. My insane thinking asked, "Was it so terrible?" At least life was exciting when I was using. I did not have the awareness of self-talk at the time, so I allowed the whispers to continue. An unchecked whisper is patient and cunning. In time it broke me down.

For years I was trapped in limbo, more of a purgatory. I had one foot in recovery and one foot in addiction. I went from full-on addict to functional addict. Going in and out of the program is torture. I knew what my life could be if I lived healthy but I couldn't get there because living healthy was so unfulfilling and uninspired.

Throughout my life, thankfully I stayed consistent when it came to reading my books on self-help and spirituality. I was one of those people who would offer unsolicited advice and solutions to everyone who crossed my path. I had all the answers, but never any actions to back up my words. When I had even the slightest amount of clean time, I turned into a preachy, patronizing person. I, of course, continued to surround myself with others like myself. They tolerated my sanctimonious behavior because they knew it was just a matter of time before I was sitting around the coffee table, passing either the straw or pipe.

As a functional addict, my cycle was get off work on Friday afternoon and go on a bender. I would have all Saturday and Sunday to be horribly sick and then go back to work on Monday. I would still be sick at work, but I was able to function somewhat. I had become a responsible drug addict, if such a thing can exist. For the most part, I never missed a car payment or rent, and I tended to have food in the fridge on a regular basis.

I was all over the map in this period of time. I had goals and started dreaming of a better life. I would go through spurts, and I would commit to improving my health, earning more money and being a better person. I would try to make up for lost time and take on a million projects at once. When the responsibilities became too much, and hard work was required, I would find a reason to run away. I would run back to my only relief I knew, as temporary as it was.

I started to climb the ladder in the fitness industry, which brought a wonderful feeling of pride within. That sense of pride in accomplishment was foreign to me. I found something that I was talented at! Finally! My workload was growing and I was able to have an assistant to help me out. I formed a great friendship bond with her; she was a person I could trust and confide in. I told her of my past, and how I was on the road to recovery. She despised the drug scene but was supportive of my cause.

While we worked closely together our friendship turned into a relationship. We lived together and then got married. She had one very strict rule: that if I ever went back to using it was over. I took this to heart and stayed clean.

My hobby of reading books on spirituality went from a hobby to an obsession. I was making breakthroughs and learning a new way of life. My life was coming together. I didn't want to ruin everything, as I had always done in the past. I still had bouts of depression and issues with my anxiety, but I held it together fairly well.

In time I found myself falling back into old thinking patterns yet again. All it takes is that whisper that I mentioned previously. If the whisper isn't silenced, it grows in strength and volume. It started with a drunk night with my buddies and one line of cocaine. The obsession took over yet again. I was very careful not to get caught. I lied and used in secret the best I could, but it was impossible not to see the changes in my health and behavior. I left the fitness industry and bounced from sales job to sales job. The boss was a prick, the company was corrupt, or my co-workers were incompetent. I had all the bases covered for when I had to move on.

I was a terrible husband and I created severe amounts of damage. Our relationship was teetering on the edge. I was so wrapped up in myself and the dope that I cared for no one unless it directly benefitted me. My wife eventually caught me using so I made every promise under the sun that it would not continue. I meant it, but we always do at the time we are saying it. I did manage to stay clean for some time and gained back some trust. We decided to have a baby. My wife had always wanted to be a mother, and I knew I would be a great dad. When my son was born, it was the best day of my life. I remember holding him and saying "I will do right by you and give you the best life possible. I will love you more than I have loved anyone in my life." Life was good for a while, but it's amazing how sleep deprivation can bring out the truth about how people feel about one another. There had been so much damage done in the past, and so many hidden resentments, that our marriage started to fall apart. When my son was six months old, we separated, and I moved into my own apartment. As you can predict, the pain of losing what I thought was going to be a lifetime relationship, the family unit, the guilt and my new-found freedom pushed me over the edge. Of course, these were all excuses to justify using again.

I was a dad, and as messed up as I was, I was determined to be the best dad ever. It was a hard go raising my son on my own. I eventually had fifty percent custody and was never going to do anything to lose that. I had to stay clean for the most part. My son needed me, and I needed him. I had never felt love like this in my life, and I never valued someone else over my own needs before. I was a fanatic when it came to boiling his bottles, and feeding him at the right time. I could change a diaper in under 10 seconds. I discovered I could put on a mesmerizing play with sock puppets and stuffed animals. It didn't matter what I wanted; it was my son calling the shots. I can remember staying up countless nights walking up and down my apartment hallway pushing him in his buggy so he would fall back asleep. I would go to work with one eye shut and the other half open because I was so exhausted. That didn't matter. I was a dad and that was everything.

There were times when I would sing the single parent's blues about how hard it was. The times I was overwhelmed I would strategically plan a bender night. I would make sure to have a couple of days to recover when I didn't have my son. I knew what I was doing was wrong, but I didn't have any real coping skills. Getting wasted was my go-to for temporary relief. After my *run away from life* bender, I would be worse off. Whatever problems I had before the binge were amplified by my using. My guilt was compounded because I knew I was risking all that I was and everything that I cared for.

I have never been under the influence while my son was in my care. I promised myself that the day he was born, and it is a promise I would rather die than break. Relapse after relapse may have discouraged me, but I wouldn't allow it to break me completely.

I wanted to be a role model, and I wanted to be a father my son could be proud of. I started filling my free time with volunteer work. This was a crucial decision on my part. It helped me get out of my head by helping others. Volunteer work made me feel like I was finally contributing, and not just a taker. It was time I paid it forward. I began exploring other methods of guidance when it came to my inner peace. I was a voracious reader. I would go through a couple of self-help books a week. The 12-step programs and attending a meeting every day was not right for me, so I was on a mission to create my own recovery program. My goal setting was constant, but I was still in the *all talk and no walk* phase. The most important part of this period was that I was planting seeds, opening my mind to possibilities, and slowly started letting go of some of the guilt I had inside. I was beginning to see I wasn't all garbage. I allowed myself to dream.

I loved my son as a baby of course, but I sure got a kick out of him when he became mobile. Every day he was with me I took him on a new adventure. I loved that he was seeing or doing things for the very first time. I was constantly planning our next outing together. Seeing his eyes light up at every new experience touched my heart. When he reached up for me and called me daddy it would make me tear up. It still does.

My home life with Alex was everything I wanted, but I was still contending with my depression, loneliness, and cravings. It was like I could put all my outside issues on pause while my son was with me but when he was with his mom, they would all come flooding back. I was still in the phase of serial dating. I constantly had a new woman in my life. Some used, and some were clean. I wanted a relationship, but I wasn't capable of being in one. I have learned over the years that a relationship is a two-way street. I still hadn't found the right coping skills that would work for me when I was upset or stressed. Whether it was a job I currently worked and hated, whatever woman problem I was having or any other obstacle real or imagined, I would find a window to go on a bender.

My life pattern became that throughout the week I was sober and clean but when I would drop my son off on Saturday at 4 pm the first thing I would do was go directly to the beer vendor. I would then call "The Man" (my drug dealer). I wouldn't have my son back until Monday so this gave me plenty of time to recover. It was to the point where my mind justified my need to use. My mind told me I wasn't doing any harm by going out and getting wasted once a week when in fact that certainly wasn't the case. If my ex-wife would have known that I was still using she would have gone for full custody, and rightfully so. I kept it my little secret. I was living two lives; during the week I was a dad, salesman, and volunteer. On the weekend, I was a full-on drug addict. I was spending time in some pretty sketchy places, with very sketchy people. Many times while I was sitting around the coffee table, knowing just how sick I was going to be, the feeling of overwhelming guilt and shame would appear and I would think to myself, *just a couple of days ago I was in a board room giving a presentation while wearing a suit.* I would then ask myself "How did this happen again?"

My "harmless" once a week benders began to take their toll on my health again. My body had had enough, and it was starting to shut down. In the past, I could use all night and still maintain my routines. When I used, I lost the ability to speak; all I could get out was a forced stutter. My body would twitch painfully when high, and my nose, ears, and throat would ache to the point of agony. The chest pains continued for days after a bender, and my nose bleeds were becoming more frequent. I had severe mood swings, and paranoia was setting in. It was not easy hiding all these side effects from my family and friends. Everyone suspected I was back in the game but they were too afraid to say anything. I would have cut them out of my life if they dared question me. I was still a horribly selfish, self-centered person. I just somehow switched those negative traits off when it came to my son. My working life was impacted by my weekly benders. I would quit or get fired because of calling in sick too often. I was broke most of the time and yet somehow managed to pay my rent, my car loan, and the other necessities of life. When I painted myself into a corner I would run back to a recovery program just to get some clean time and hide from the havoc I had created. I would bring it to the brink, where I was about to lose everything, then take some action to save it. I knew, however, it was just a matter of time before I would slide back into hell, and I was very aware of this. I wanted to get better and stay better but nothing I tried worked. I started to lose all hope. I needed a miracle.

My miracle moment appeared! My son and I were walking down the hallway of our apartment. He was still quite young and took his time waddling his way to the door in his snow suit. I was rushing a bit, and I ended up taking a few steps ahead of him. I guess this scared him because he said something to me that changed my life forever. He said, "Daddy, don't leave me." This rocked me to the core. It forced my mind to realize that if I died I would be leaving him behind. My understanding of how badly he needed his daddy brought tears to my eyes, and a new strength that I desperately needed. I heard a voice in my head say "Whatever it takes" and I knew I had to do whatever it took to be there for my son. At the same time, the solution came to me. I was going to take all that I had learned over the years from the recovery programs (that I agreed with) and combine them with all that I gained from the books I had read on self-help and spirituality. Next, I was going to look for a new method of help. I am a firm believer that if you have the right mindset and take action you will attract what you need into your life. Shortly after this life-altering moment a friend called me and mentioned that he was going to check out a counseling program through the United Way. (I didn't know at the time it was a United Way program.) I immediately phoned and made an

appointment. The counseling was exactly what I needed. We talked about my past and my way of thinking. This opened up new doors to my perception. It was the final piece of the puzzle. I wish I could say that I never used again but that wouldn't be true. I spent years of trial and error perfecting my own system of recovery. I would have a slip here and there but could recover fast, and went right back to the drawing board. I would identify where I went wrong, and find a solution. The simple solution was to follow my program like my life depended on it, because it did. Any time I would start slacking and let down my guard I was opening the door to my old way of thinking. I understood that any bad habit must be replaced by a good one. It takes time and repetition to change old ingrained thought patterns.
As my attitude changed so did the quality of my life. I looked at the people I had in my life and starting making cuts. The people that brought more harm than good were phased out. My self-talk was carefully monitored, and any crazy thinking was shifted into empowering thoughts.

One of the biggest turning points in my life was at a Rotary Club meeting. I had been a volunteer there for a while and attended a regular lunch function. At each function there was a guest speaker. On this particular day, we had the pleasure of hearing a motivational speaker. This spitfire of a woman spoke for 20 minutes on her life, and regaled us with her challenges and victories. I felt the energy in the room rise. She was glowing with positivity and a genuine interest in helping others. As she was speaking, I felt something click inside. This was my calling; this is what I was meant to do. I felt such a weight off my shoulders. I had found my purpose. After she was finished, she directed us to the back of the room where her book was for sale. I, of course, bought it and read it immediately. As I was reading it, I felt that connection to my calling again. I knew I was going to write a book. I was inspired and on fire!

Motivation and inspiration can fade fast unless nurtured. After a few short hours, I went into an inner darkness. The voices in my head mocked me, saying "You are a failure and you always will be. Who do you think you are, that you could help and inspire others? You are too stupid to write a speech, never mind a book. If you try to get up in front of a crowd and speak, you will forget what to say and everyone will laugh at your attempt. Why put yourself through this humiliation? Accept that you're a junkie and a write-off. Go back to your miserable life and run out the clock. You are nothing and will amount to nothing." Usually, this kind of thought pattern would send me back to the old way of coping. Not this time! I finally took a stand. I reached out to the speaker. I told her of my past and what my future aspirations were. She asked me to speak at an event she hosted called MoMonday (Motivation Mondays). This event was a dinner, with five different speakers who would go on stage for ten minutes each. It was a broad range of talks that would inspire and motivate others. I immediately accepted, hung up the phone and vomited. I knew this was my path, so I was going to do whatever it took. I had a few months to prepare, so I went after it. This was the first time in my life where procrastination was not an option. I wrote one hell of a great speech, and I practiced it every day, right up until the big day. When I was called up on stage, I was shaking and terrified. The event was completely sold out, and I had never stood in front of this many people ever. They had a huge spotlight on, which temporarily blinded me. I was handed a microphone, and off I went. My hard work and practice kicked in, and I did my thing. I didn't hold the mic close enough to my mouth, and I stammered in a few spots, but overall I did a great job. Overcoming my fear, working hard and finding the courage to put myself out there was the biggest accomplishment of my life. All of this felt great, but what confirmed my calling was the reaction I received from the audience. People were crying, cheering and coming up to hug me. I did something to connect to others and it felt so right.

When the evening was over I was on a well-earned natural high. I knew who I was and who I was to become. Now it was time to improve on every other aspect of my life.

One of the biggest issues in my life was my work. I was in yet another sales job that I despised. It literally sucked the life out of me. I was well aware that it was going to take time and hard work to gain the skills needed to be a paid speaker. I needed to find a way that I could start to make real money, but still enjoy a quality of life that I believed in. I needed money coming in so I could continue to chase my dreams of becoming a speaker/author; I had no formal education or any high-end skills to offer, so I was stumped as to what to do.

The concept of multi-level marketing was introduced to me by someone who was making a great living at it. I wasn't sure what to make of it, but I admired the lifestyle and wanted it for myself. I was under the misguided impression that MLMs were all scams and pyramid schemes. I did the research and discovered that MLM is the future, and I did not want to miss the boat in life once again. I loved the idea of being an entrepreneur. If I did the work and persevered, there would be no limit to my income. Blaming others for my lack of earnings was no longer an option. I took the plunge and started working at MLM part time. My business took off. I was climbing the ranks fast. I worked hard, and in a short period of time, money starting coming in. For the first time in a long time, I wasn't constantly stressed about money. I hated my full-time job but with the way things were going, I would be able to quit shortly. Things were going so great that I started to coast. I believed I had my life in order, so I stopped taking my life program seriously and I put my MLM business on auto pilot. I felt I had worked it hard enough and that it would keep going on its own. This was a costly mistake. With my guard down and my arrogance level at an all-time high, I started making bad choices. I had grown accustomed to a certain quality of life and health. I took it for granted and stopped putting in the work. If you're not growing, you're dying. Life always has interesting ways to either get you back on track or break you. My MLM business flatlined. I was allowing negative thoughts to control my outlook, and my cravings for the dope scene intensified.

All I can say is F**k That!!! All of this happening was actually a huge blessing. I had come so far there was no way I was going to throw it all away. I refused to live my life as a fraud. How could I possibly help anyone if I wasn't living my life right? I had a calling and nothing was going to stop me from answering. Suffering is a great motivator, and humility is the great equalizer. I had put in so many years of work on myself that it was natural to make the shift back to the person I was meant to be. I knew I was still going to make mistakes in the future, but this setback was what I needed. If I didn't fail, then I wasn't trying. If I didn't fail, I would never learn or grow.

I knew I had the right belief system, the right attitude, and an insatiable work ethic. I started taking action that began the momentum. All of a sudden the right people started coming into my life. I realized that the MLM I was previously involved in wasn't the right one for me. I could see myself with a different company, but I had no idea where to start looking. All I knew was MLM was going to be a big part of my future. As the law of attraction would have it, someone I knew from way back contacted me with an MLM opportunity. I am grateful every day that he took the time to bring me in and help me get things going. It was a simple concept that would help people with their health and their finances. I jumped in with both feet. I started working every free moment I could. My priority, of course, was my son. When he was with me it was daddy and son time. When he was sleeping I was working, and when he was with his mom I was working. Any free moment I had outside of my dreaded day job, I was working my business. I finally made a move from one full-time sales job to another, only to find I despised it just as much as the last one, but that wasn't going to get me down. There was nothing wrong with the jobs I was working; they just were not something that I was passionate about. What kept me going was knowing that one day I would be free to leave the noose of the corporate life and fly free as an entrepreneur. I learned that "to be successful you must be willing to do the things today that others won't do in order to have the things tomorrow others won't have" – Les Brown. When I heard that saying

I knew I had to get up extra early and stay up late in order to do the things that needed to be done, whether I felt like it or not. I also knew I was going to dedicate my life to showing people that they are capable of this as well. With the right support and the right mindset everyone can follow their calling.

I also started working on my ultimate goal as I mentioned earlier - to be a motivational speaker and author. I joined a variety of Toastmasters groups and started learning the skills that I needed in order to deliver a great speech. I took on numerous speaking gigs for the practice and, wow, did I need it. I really stunk. If I wasn't the one on stage speaking, I probably would have stood up and left myself. In the words of Les Brown, my body stood up, and my brain sat down. I have had some incredibly embarrassing moments in my speaking career. I remember one time when I went on stage, I just stood there with a vacant look in my eyes until an audience member yelled are you going to start talking or what? On another occasion I tripped and did a face plant on the steps on my way to the stage. Another time I was so nervous that I sweated through my shirt, and you could clearly see that I had huge sweat stains under my arms. Embarrassing! I may have been a sweaty, clumsy guy that forgot what to say, but I was also a man on a mission that would never stop trying.

Next, I began to write my book. This was such a terrifying prospect. The idea of reliving my past was not something I relished. Even harder was the idea to put it out there for all the world to see. I had made the decision to do it, so I would have to get over the humiliation of what my story entails and whatever possible repercussions that might surface from my past. I owed it to myself and to anyone that might benefit from what I have learned from my experiences. I figured I had failed at nearly everything in life, so it was relevant to a wide variety of people. The question was how does a guy with learning issues and the equivalency of a grade nine education write a book? (Remember, high school is still a blur to me.) The answer was that if I was to write from my heart with the intent of helping others I could do it! I also gave myself some credit knowing that I had been an avid reader for years, and that I had learned a great deal along my journey. I, of course, would need help with the actual editing and publishing, but this didn't concern me because I knew the solution would present itself if I put in the work.

Life was starting to happen for me! All of my dreams were starting to come true. I could finally see the light at the end of this long tunnel. This was when life sent me yet again a few more curve balls. It is easy to be positive in life when things are going your way, but the real test is when life throws those curve balls!

First, I was fired from the sales job that I worked at full-time during the day. I am the first to say I deserved to be fired, and they probably should have gotten rid of me long before this. I was very motivated at everything in my life, with the exception of my sales job. My attitude was awful. I tried everything in my arsenal to see the positive attributes of working there, but all I could do was make things up. My life was heading in the direction of honesty. I tried to make up things I enjoyed about working there, but they just weren't true. This attitude reflected in my performance. I just couldn't bring myself to fake laugh at a joke that wasn't funny. I couldn't pretend what I was selling was exciting because it bored me to tears. I could no longer go along to get along. The owner of the company took me in his office to give me the axe. It took all I had to not jump up and hug him. I need to point out the issue was with me, not with the company I worked for. I was ceremoniously walked off the premises by two people. The old Dan would have made a grand exit by throwing things off people's desks and kicking over a plant. The real Dan smiled, shook hands with anyone around, and said goodbye with a smile. However, the second I got in my car I went into a panic! *How am I going to pay for my rent? How am I going to support my boy? I'm doomed!* These fears passed as quickly as they came. I started singing in my car at the top of my lungs "I got fired!" Thank you universe! I am finally free to live the life I was meant to live.

Second, yet another relationship failed, which was no surprise to me. I had been in many relationships over the years that either exploded or imploded. I may have said the word forever, but deep down I didn't believe it. I constantly did things to sabotage whatever relationship I was in. I would piss off my partner's friends or try to change the person into what I wanted them to be. I was controlling with some and didn't care for others. I had the mindset that my way of doing things was right and everyone else was wrong. I was in a perpetual state of judgment, which is ridiculous for someone with my track record. Anyone who questioned my motives was perceived as a threat and expelled from my life. It is impossible to be in a healthy relationship when you are not healthy yourself. I knew I needed to take the time and get to know the single life for a while. I had always needed someone in my life, almost like a security blanket. I knew that if I became right within myself, I would attract the right person into my life.

I started focusing on how I felt inside, who I was and who I wanted to become. I made my living program (which I will share with you later in the book) my number one priority. I finally understood that working on myself was crucial if I wanted to live the life I had always dreamed of. After an extended period of self-discovery and a strict regimen of positivity, things began to happen.

While attending a Winnipeg Chambers of Commerce business meeting I had the honor of hearing a speaker from the United Way. She spoke of overcoming her depression, and the help that she received from the United Way. When she spoke she was so compelling that I rushed up and hugged her when she was done. I knew at that moment I was meant to join the United Way volunteer speakers group. I reviewed my recovery history to find out one of the programs that I had experienced in my past that had a pivotal effect on me was through the United Way. I had no idea. There are no coincidences in life, and this was a meant to be kind of thing. You can only imagine how proud I was when my story was featured as part of their major fundraising campaign! I now dedicate a great deal of my free time to speak at different functions in order to raise awareness of the programs the United Way offers.

The right girl came into my life at the right time, because I was finally ready within. She supports my dreams and I hers. I always thought it was cheesy when I heard people say their partners were their best friends. I get it now. There have been many extreme ups and downs during our time together, but we always know we can count on each other. We live together, out in the country, with my son and her two daughters. We are a happily dysfunctional family. There is nothing more inspiring than working towards your goals together as a team. We have huge aspirations for the future.

I met a fellow entrepreneur and we decided to go into a business venture together. Another one of those "meant to be" moments was that one of my fellow partners within this company owned a publishing firm. I explained to him my lifelong dream about writing a book. I clarified the content and my vision. He immediately encouraged me and went out of his way to help with the process. I have the utmost respect for anyone that can make sense and organize the grammatical disaster that I submitted.

I decided I wanted to improve my health. I posted a request on Facebook to see if anyone had an elliptical gathering dust that they would like to sell. An incredibly energetic British fella answered my request and told me to come by his place to pick up the machine. When I arrived I was greeted by him and his wife, and made an immediate connection. It turns out they were already involved in one of the businesses I was involved in. We decided to work together as a team. This was a life-changing moment as it opened up doors and truly launched my business. This is an excellent example of how, when preparation and opportunity meet, the potential is limitless. If I hadn't been working as hard as I was and living the way I was they would never have seen my potential. The result was I acquired my health machine, but more importantly, I met two extraordinary people that became real lifelong friends and business partners.

Out of the blue I felt compelled to express my gratitude to my friend that hosts the MoMonday show in Winnipeg. I had to make her aware of how much of an impact she had on my life since I met her and heard her speak. I let her know what I had been doing with my life since meeting her and how I would never have known my mission if I had not been given the opportunity to be on the show. Her response floored me. She asked me not only to go on her radio show to talk about my book, but she also invited me to speak on stage for MoMonday again!

My family and friends now see me in a different light. I have spent the majority of my life sick and selfish. A large amount of damage was done, but over the years I have started to gain back the trust and respect I lost. It's been a long time since I have seen that fear and worry in my parents' eyes, and that means the world to me. I believe I am becoming the kind of son a parent can be proud of, and the kind of father a son can look up to. My journey is just beginning! I have massive goals, and most revolve around helping others. No matter how hard the challenges become, there will always be a way. I am all out of excuses. All that is left are my dreams, which will become a reality!

Have you ever asked yourself "Is this all there is? Is this my life?"

These are questions I had asked myself many times. They came to my mind more frequently after I had cleaned up and settled in for a "normal life." I know that I asked these questions many times in my excuse-accepting days. Getting up to go to a job I despised, fighting traffic on the way to and from work, feeling exhausted and stressed, only to come home to sit down, have a meal, watch TV and then go to bed early just so I could get up and do it all over again. Living the same day over and over again. I would wait desperately for the weekend to come, when I was granted a slight reprieve from the everyday routine. I always felt that the week was a write-off for enjoyment. On weekends there were chores to do, and preparation for the upcoming work week. I would hope for a window within that time to do something that was fun, but it was rare. I always had a feeling of unease and unrest because I knew that there was a better life out there, but I was constantly using every excuse in my arsenal as to why it wasn't possible for me. What if I now decided that it was time for a change? I started to realize that time was running out! I knew deep down that if I didn't make my move now, I would die empty and full of regrets. The next question was... "What is my first step to fulfillment and a greater life?!"

The first step in overcoming any excuse is to identify it. Some excuses have been repeated so many times that they have become part of us, and therefore they are not easily detectable. Once you identify and bring these excuses to the forefront of your mind, they will be exposed for the frauds that they are. The goal is to set a mental security system that is full of sensors. Anything remotely close to an excuse should be red flagged and immediately scrutinized. To maintain a mental security system requires discipline, constant vigilance, and repetition. Once you have the security system as a daily routine it will become second nature.

Here are some excuse category examples that will set off the siren within your security system. Please note that every example and every category is fear, in many different versions and forms.

Chapter 1

Family, Friends, But Most Of All Strangers Own Me

People live their lives in constant fear of what a complete stranger may think or say about them. This is a prime excuse for not being the person you truly are. This fear has been ingrained and programmed into our minds from the beginning of our childhood. It seems as though the planet is obsessed with the thoughts and opinions of strangers over everything else, even their family, and friends. It's bizarre that lives are lived and altered by the mere hint of another person's possible disapproval. Often creating scenarios of perceived thought, a stranger can make a person take drastic action on their quest for acceptance.

When I was in grade school, one of the biggest atrocities that could occur to a young man trying to find himself in the world happened to me. Now keep in mind that a young fella has to act like a tough guy in front of his fellow mates, and be a rebel who is dangerous and exciting for the girls. This is a standard that is hard to maintain at the best of times, but when you wake up in the morning with a huge pimple on the end of your nose, it truly is the end of the world. Yes, of course, we as adults realize how trivial such a thing is (or do we?). But at this time in my life all social order was at stake. My parents were teachers and I didn't think that they would find a blemish on my face a viable reason to be truant for the week while I waited for the monstrosity to clear up and vacate the premises. It was essential that drastic action had to be taken!

My first course of action in order to stay home from school was standard and guaranteed. I, of course, chewed up a bunch of Chips Ahoy cookies, made lots of moaning and choking noises while dramatically spitting them into the toilet. My parents, seeing that I was physically ill, sent me back to bed for the day. This gave me time to scheme up a way to spend the rest of the week in the comfort of a non-judgmental sanctuary. I was so worried that I would have to go to school the next day, to be scrutinized by my peers, that I became literally sick to my stomach. The fear of what other people thought of me made me physically sick, paranoid, irrational and borderline psychotic. The funny thing was that when my mom came home from work that day, she brought me a large number of medicines to help bring me back to proper health… and all I really needed was a tube of Clearasil.

In my adult years, I lived in constant fear of my intellect being called into question. I cringed at the idea of anyone thinking of me as a stupid person. Because I had learning disabilities I always thought that meant I was stupid. (I should point out that using your learning disability as a way of getting out of doing the work is yet another excuse. Investing your time and hard work opens the door to continued learning opportunities.) Because of the fact that I was so paranoid of what others thought of me, I was on guard at all times. I was terrified I would do or say something that would make people laugh at me.

I attended an "adult" party that consisted mainly of successful and sophisticated people. My nerves were on the edge and my self-esteem was at an all-time low. I was listening to them speak about politics and the state of the planet. I instantly despised these people, and knew that they were getting ready to unleash a stream of mockery that would burn me to the core of my soul. When someone suggested a spirited game of Trivial Pursuit I had just about had it. Better to have them think me as an oaf rather than an idiot, so I took action. I have always been prone to theatrics so I had a great idea as to how I could end this disastrous idea. I tripped and spilled an enormous glass of rye and coke all over the game board. I, of course, was beside myself with embarrassment and apologies, and a sly inner smile that knew the Trivial Pursuit game had to be regretfully canceled for the evening. Wow! Looking back I see how insane it was to come up with such a crazy idea as ruining the game board, just because of what other people might have thought of me!

As adults, you would think that we would have clued into how detrimental the effects are of living a life dominated by the possible opinions of others. You would think that after all the suffering and insecurities that played such a role in our childhood, we would have learned that to please the masses and expect approval from everyone in our lives leads to nothing but unhappiness and misery. Unfortunately, our fear of what others think tends to increase as we get older. It is as simple as looking around you and seeing how people are so obsessed with the clothing that they are wearing, the houses that they live in, and the cars that they drive. People dictate their value based on the way they look, the things they own, and their titles in life. There is so much emphasis on our outward appearances and our possessions. Such little effort is made to our own personal growth and happiness. If we spent just a fraction of the time on how we feel inside as opposed to what other people think about what they see on the "outside," life would be so much more peaceful.

Many people say they don't care what others think, but I hear them say this with a defensive attitude. In reality, the ones who protest the most are usually the ones who are living in the most fear.

A real hard cold fact is that no matter how you look, what you say or how you act, people are going to think the way they think, no matter what, and there is absolutely nothing that you can do about it.

I once heard a speaker talk about how to deal with our fears of what people may think of us. He spoke about when we die. He mentioned that on average only ten people will physically cry at a funeral service.

Can you imagine? You're living on this planet, working your whole life, interacting with thousands of other human beings, to have only ten people mourn you so deeply that they physically cry? He went on to say that the weather can dictate the actual burial attendance. The weather! If it's raining out it is said that 50% of the procession will drop out. Their short-term comfort is more important than your whole life on this earth! Now keep in mind these are the actions of people that know you and care about you. If this is what can be expected from people who know us, why the hell would we remotely care about what some stranger may think of us? The fact is that most people are just so self-absorbed that they are too focused on themselves to even notice if you're having a bad hair day. All of this may seem morbid but it's not; it's a very liberating revelation. Now that we have this firmly in our minds we are not a hostage to anyone! We no longer care about what other people think or say about us. We are now free to look, act and feel the way we genuinely believe we should, and we can do it without fear. Imagine how wonderful your life can be, now that you refuse to be owned by anyone else's thoughts.

The "I'm worried about what others may think of me" excuse has been identified. Set your mental alarm and refuse to let another person's thoughts, whether they are real or imagined, own you! When this particular fear or excuse comes to my mind, I take great pleasure in yelling NO ONE OWNS ME!

Chapter 2

But Everyone In My Life Lives This Way!

Most of us have heard the old saying "You are who you surround yourself with." This is a true statement. If you surround yourself with people who are negative, unhappy or underachievers who lack ambition, then there is an excellent chance that you're going to live your life this way as well. We have a choice of whom we allow in our lives, and this dictates who we are today and who we will be in the future. It's very easy to stay in an unhappy, safe rut. It's very hard to break away from the instability of a lesser life. When a person is finally making their breakaway from these types of people, they tend to have to drop the majority of their family and friends, who are not like-minded. This is a very hard thing to do, as people fear change and can be severely threatened by it.

It amazes me what great lengths some people will go through to drag you back down to where you once were. They are living in quiet desperation. They are threatened by the progress in another person because it forces them to truly look within themselves. The people that you are not compelled to release from your life are usually some family members or close friends. A great deal of inner strength is required because it is not unheard of for a family member or a close friend to try to sabotage your efforts. They are in a state of fear of losing you because you are on a path of personal growth while they are staying static. This is where the hard decisions come in. It can be painful to extricate someone who has been in your life for a long time, but it is very simple to decide who should be in your life and who should not. A simple test is to look at each and every single person who is in your life, and think about how they make you feel when you are with them. When you are in their presence, does your energy level go up? Or does it go down? Do you feel happy, inspired and at peace? Or do you feel tired, anxious and defeated? Negative people can be compared to cancer. If these damaging people are not excised, they can poison your whole mind, body and spirit.

In the past, I spent the majority of my time with people who were using drugs and had no real aspirations in life. People who cared little for themselves, never mind others. No matter how hard I tried to better myself, I stayed within that same mindset because I was surrounded by it. Upon reflection, I realized I never had a chance to get clean and to be able to stay that way, with the people in my life. Every point of contact was drug-related. Every conversation consisted of either how desperately my friends wanted to get high or how sick they were at that moment.

When you are in a particular surrounding long enough, you accept it as normal. I went through most of my life thinking it was just a part of life to be horribly sick 4 or 5 times a week, to miss work (if I was working) on a regular basis, or to spend all the money I could get my hands on and not have enough money for necessities. Old habits and old thinking patterns are very easy to fall back into, as it's what we know. It becomes our "normal." We wear blinders to what we have in our lives and what we think is acceptable. It's only when we become aware that we come out of the fog and see things for what they truly are.

The moment we become conscious of the total impact of our surroundings is when we can start to take the steps to a new life. I had to eliminate the majority of the people in my life and start from scratch. It was my realization that it is better to have no one in my life than to have those people who affected me in a way that I couldn't feel happiness or have any positive direction. With the right mindset and the courage to move forward I sought out like-minded people. My quality of life grew in time, and the opportunities and experiences through the people that I met began to present themselves.

The "everyone else is doing that" (or not doing that) excuse has been identified. Set your mental alarm for any inner talk of what is and what is not right for you, based on how others in your life are living their lives.

Chapter 3

Why Don't You Shut Your Mouth? My Attitude Is Fine

A lot of people are miserable, bitter and angry. These people are looking to spread their misery. They use every excuse in the book to justify their unhappiness. Something as basic as the weather can send people into an absolute state of gloom.

I was one of those people. Keep in mind I live in Winnipeg, Manitoba, Canada. Also known as Winterpeg. Our winters are very long and frigid most of the time. I used this as an excuse, and would always complain about my quality of life. The first sign of snowfall was the end of the world as I knew it. I have said on numerous occasions that my life is over for the next eight months because hell was coming. I hated the cold! A bit dramatic, I admit, but this was how I honestly felt because my attitude and outlook about winter was so despondent. I allowed my view to call it quits for most of the year. I would refuse to leave the house, and sequestered myself as best I could until the summer brought me back to life. I now reflect on all that I missed out on, and how selfish I was behaving. I thought this way for over 20 years, before I changed my thoughts to how I should maybe dress a bit more warmly and then perhaps it wouldn't be so bad. I started to look at all the positive things that winter had to offer. Simple solutions were right in front of my nose, but my attitude blinded me. I had grown accustomed to my self-pity and my hibernation patterns. I still need to say that I do not magically enjoy the cold just because I put on another sweater. I would take a day at the beach in a heartbeat over any day in the snow! The difference now is I can still be happy all year round because I have decided to be happy. Another way that I look at it is I can take the action needed to leave this frozen tundra to a climate more acceptable to my needs.

You can always determine a person's attitude by how they speak of others. I used to thrive on speaking poorly of other people, and how they were living their lives wrong. I would pick out any character flaw I felt they had. I did this, of course, because I had such low self-esteem. I would root around in other people's failures to pump up my ego. I had zero consideration for others, and the reasons why they behaved the way they did. I have a history of being a major gossip, and full of judgment. When I finally became aware of my attitude I started correcting it. I stopped receiving calls from people saying "I heard what you said about me!" Those were the worst calls. Keep in mind that whoever you are gossiping to is more than likely gossiping about you as well. There is no honor amongst the people who find fault in everyone else. Break free of talking trash, and cut out the people that are trash talkers from your life.

Let's face it. Attitude is everything! It dictates the quality of our lives. Our attitude is what controls our level of happiness or sadness, and I have found that a simple change of attitude can make a world of difference. We can decide how we feel about people, places or things in our life. We can allow challenging situations to break us down and bring us further pain. When someone has a bad attitude, it's like being in a black hole of negativity. No one wants to be around someone who is always complaining about their lives. People with bad attitudes tend to offend people, and are avoided by most.

I love the saying "When you change the way you look at things, the things you look at change."- Wayne Dyer. When I began writing this book I was overwhelmed with fear, self-doubt, and trepidation. This made the actual process in the beginning more like a chore than a sense of pleasure. When I adjusted my attitude, everything changed.

I thought to myself, this is my opportunity to help other people and to help myself. The writing process became exciting and fun again.

I have come across so many people with such bad attitudes, who are always complaining about their lives. It's almost like they feed on pain. I find that even having a conversation with a complete stranger, the majority of the time the conversation leads to some negative story in the paper or on the news. For some reason, people seem to gravitate to what is going wrong and not what's going right. I have also learned that when you try to flip the conversation to something positive, the person either becomes offended or directs it back to yet another negative situation.

Our attitudes are so powerful that they can control our health. People I know who have awful attitudes tend to be sick often; they are easily stressed or they feel unfulfilled in their work and personal life.

Our attitudes in the workplace have a huge bearing on our success level. How many times, when speaking with a co-worker about "living the dream," have you heard them say this in such a sarcastic manner in order to relay their true feelings about their current position? Bad attitudes are so easily sensed by most. They come off people in waves. People with bad attitudes send off a vibe that is felt by all. You can literally feel the misery surrounding them.

Our attitudes have a profound effect on our family. When you come home from work and your partner asks you how your day was, and you go off on a tangent about how incompetent fellow employees or the management staff are, then continue to vent about how bad traffic was, how little you earn, how worried you are about the bills or how scared you are for the future, it can cause the people around you to become unhappy as well. Our attitudes set the stage for everyone that is connected to us. Your family is at home, happy and enjoying their lives, and you can take that away from them in an instant by having such a negative attitude.

I've heard the phrase "Be grateful for what you have" many times. No one likes to be told things like that when they are in a bad state of mind. The question is, how do we change our attitude? The first thing you have to do is identify and become aware of what your attitude usually is. Then you must decide whether you care enough about yourself and your loved ones to change your attitude. I provide suggestions on how we can change our way of thinking and our attitude in the latter part of this book, but I can say that being aware of your attitude, along with the willingness to change, are the critical ingredients to a happier life.

The "bad attitude" excuse has been identified. Set your mental alarm. The moment you start looking for fault, sharing negative thoughts, or have the urge to complain, take a step back. Realize that thinking and voicing such negative views only harms yourself. Happiness attracts happiness.

Chapter 4

What's The Rush?
I Have Plenty Of Time

Wow! This excuse is readily accepted and used by almost everyone I know. How does anyone know what time we have left in order to accomplish anything? There is never such a thing as guaranteed time! Millions of people who have had the best intentions for tomorrow didn't make it through the night. Procrastination is subtle and yet lethal when it comes to letting life pass us by. I have been a master procrastinator for the majority of my life. I attribute this to my severe lack of confidence and my addiction to instant gratification.

I spent close to two decades of hell, putting off getting healthy. I can remember at the tender age of 18 thinking *I have my whole life ahead of me. I have nothing but time. I don't have to worry about getting a career, a home or planning for my future. What's the big rush? I can party and have a ton of fun for a while and I will start thinking about my future later.* Having this attitude robbed me of most of my adult life.

I would think *I know I am sick with addiction, but I am not ready to get real help and do the work.* Many of my friends shared this same attitude, and now they are dead and buried.

Several, if not most, procrastinators revel in mapping their ideas out. They will spend the lion share of their day planning what is to be done and how it will be done. They take great pride in visualizing the outcome but will never take the first step towards reaching any of their professed objectives. I have many years of daytimers filled out in full, stating my goals, hopes, and dreams. Now looking back, I immediately realize that each goal was pushed back to another date in the future. The most joy comes from a task that has enough power to make you procrastinate, but rest assured this will bring you the most satisfaction when you do complete it.

"Procrastination" is an excuse which is now identified. Set your mental alarm the moment you think that you will do it later. This is your code red alert! The second this mental alarm goes off you must come to the realization that every day, minute or even second you put your dreams or aspirations on hold will cause you much greater pain and discomfort in the long run. The pain becomes more intense the closer you get to the deadline that you set for yourself. Your life is no longer enjoyable during this procrastination period. You could be engaging in an activity that would normally bring you joy, but if you're stuck in the crunch time, you will feel nothing but stress. Whenever I catch myself procrastinating I remember a quote; "The pain of regret is far worse than the pain of discipline." Nathan Whitley

Chapter 5

I Don't Know How! Do It For Me!

We live in a new world era, where information is so easily attainable yet we still see many people looking for the easy way out. Not even trying to expand their minds, refusing to do anything on their own. It seems that they need someone to continuously hold their hand. This was certainly the case for me. I found every single way possible to have someone do the work for me. This began as far back as grade school because I had such a tough time and I didn't understand things as fast as everyone else. I was horrible at retaining any sort of information, and my work ethic was questionable at best! I spent the majority of my day in school making deals with my fellow students. I would arrange for someone to do my homework and I would always come up with elaborate ways to cheat on tests. I would have to say some of my cheating methods were borderline brilliant! The effort and thought processes that it took me to conduct and oversee these missions were complicated and fraught with risk. The stress I felt coordinating such events was taxing, and the worry of being ratted out post exam was unnerving. I could have avoided all this nonsense by just studying harder and actually believing in myself.

I didn't realize the damage this behavior would cause, and how I would become so reliant on having others do the work for me! I lacked initiative and the confidence to do anything on my own, and I carried this behavior far into my future years. There are many people, like myself, who cannot handle even the most basic tasks in life, whether going grocery shopping, getting a driver's license, or even paying bills.

It is an absolute necessity to be able to have the skills and ethics to do the work on your own. It allows you to feel pleasure and a sense of pride. Reflecting upon my past, I realize now that I put a great deal more effort into having other people do the work, than what was needed to get the job done in the first place. The "do it for me" people will eventually burn bridges with the "I'll do it for you" people in their lives. People only have so much patience, and are willing to only do so much! The "do it for me" people often travel from group to group, friendship to friendship, and have fractured families because of their constant need to be taken care of.

There is nothing wrong with not knowing how to do something new. It is very empowering to take that first step to acquire the knowledge needed on your own. Simply, just start the ball rolling. Look for the answers on your own first. If you are not able to understand things right away, that's okay! Now take the next step and ask for help. Keep in mind that there are billions of people on this planet. Somewhere someone is willing to help you, not to complete things for you but to share information and provide their guidance. It is just a matter of reaching out for help, making the call, or just a few simple clicks of your mouse. Look at what task or idea you're trying to accomplish and research who has succeeded at this and emulate their actions! There is no harm in sending out a message to that person; you would be surprised at how often I have received positive responses with offers of help.

The "I don't know how" excuse has been identified. Set your mental alarm. If you don't know how to do something, do the work required to learn, or find someone who is willing to teach you, not do the work for you.

Chapter 6

I'm WAAAAy Too Old Or WAAAAy Too Young

These are fall back excuses seemingly used by all age groups.

When I was in my early twenties, I dreamed of becoming a teacher. A teacher who could guide people to a spiritual evolution, higher living and success. My mind told me that was just not possible. My excuse was that I was too young and no one would take me seriously if I tried to teach them a new way of life. I gave up without even starting because of the age excuse. I sometimes reflect on where I would be now if I had disallowed that self-defeating inner talk. I can't change the past, but I can create my future. I will never be too young to chase a dream again.

As I got older, I started setting my limitations on what I thought I could do, based on pure fear and my outright laziness. I have passed up a multitude of opportunities. I wanted to run the Half Manitoba Marathon for many years but I kept telling myself that I was too old. I am only forty-three. Some people run marathons well into their seventies and beyond. It takes a huge amount of commitment and effort to run any marathon, especially for someone who has never done it. The sense of accomplishment would be epic. I have committed to do the run in the summer of 2017. I will be forty-four and proud that I no longer allowed life and experiences to pass me by just because of my age.

Human beings have the ability to achieve amazing things. It's just a matter of having the right belief system. When anyone falls back on the age excuse, they are saying that the goal just isn't that important to them, they fear what other people will think, or let's face it, they are lazy.

In the past I would get really angry at anyone who said you're only as old as you feel, but I now have to admit they were right. How I feel is completely up to me! Whatever goals I set now will not be age dependent.

The "age" excuse has now been identified. Set your mental alarm. Age will no longer be a factor in setting and achieving life goals.

Chapter 7

I Have No Bucks, No Connections, And No Help

This is a very popular excuse, one I have heard over and over from multitudes of people and from the voices in my head. This excuse kills a wide variety of dreams.

My dream, in particular, was owning my own business.

My excuse was that I thought I couldn't start a business, I didn't have any money and I couldn't possibly know anyone who would want to join me in my venture.

What I found that interested me the most was Multi-Level Marketing. I figured, what harm could come from at least looking into it? Even though I didn't have, what I thought, were the necessities to become an entrepreneur. I also thought, what was stopping me from acquiring them? I like the phrase "If nothing changes, nothing changes" so I started taking action through small steps. Hard work and patience is the key! As time went on, the right people and new opportunities started to present themselves to me. Every small step created more momentum and inspiration. I was putting in the work and because of this I could see the progress increasing, and along with this so did my confidence! With this confidence aura, I found that more and more people wanted to be a part of my ventures. I went from nothing to building a respectable business.

If you ever use the excuse I don't have the money, connections or support, you're not alone. I have heard it many times. Hell, I used it myself! When someone says this to me, I can almost see the light dim in their eyes. When I hear that they have always dreamed of traveling, owning a home, a nice car or starting their own business, but they say this with the attitude of never achieving these dreams. These people have given up without even making an attempt. Stop robbing yourself of the possibilities! Things may not happen overnight, but they can transpire if you take that first step. Hurry to make the decision to do the work, but be patient for the results. Keeping the right mindset, being persistent and consistently moving forward is what you will need to do in order to open those doors. I found that the person I became while reaching for my goals made me the happiest.

The "I have no money, no connections and no help" excuse has been identified. Set your mental alarm. If you don't have any of these, take a different action! Small steps will create results!

Chapter 8

My Mind Is Open To Change, As Long As I Don't Have To Do Anything Different

There are plenty of people who want a different quality of life. You've heard them. They talk about what they want to do, what they want to buy, and many more different "wants" all the time. I too spent a considerable portion of my life in that mode. I was "all talk and no action." I was so incredibly set in my ways. I professed that I had an open mind, but I didn't. I would read and research all the rituals of people who have achieved great successes in their lives, but I would quickly put these goals to bed because I believed they wouldn't work for me. I have heard many times "If you keep doing what you have been doing, you will keep getting what you have been getting." Also in many recovery programs, they say doing the same thing over and over again then expecting different results is a form of insanity.

If we want change, we must be willing to try new things, but with the right attitude of course! This takes hard work and you must be very committed. Over the years I had to use the trial and error system to see what would work for me. If one method didn't work for me I would move on to something else. I never gave up trying. The fear of change will rob us of growth and new experiences. When you open your mind to new ideas and methods and then begin to implement them, you will move forward in your life. Even if you have given it an honest try and it hasn't worked out, you are still ahead of the game. You have experienced something new and proven to yourself that you are capable of trying something different. On your continued quest of action and openness, you will find what suits you best, and the benefits are life-changing. The exciting thing is when you make your move and get out of your comfort zone it will make you feel more alive. Our minds love to be challenged, and love to feel the benefits of growth. When you have an open mind and are willing to try different things, you evolve as a person, and a whole new world of opportunities will open for you. When your mind starts to say that trying will be too hard, try focusing on the potential benefits that you will enjoy when you finally get what you want or where you want to be. That will be enough to get past the fear and laziness rut. The more you accomplish, the more you will stay motivated to press on and take on more new challenges.

The "talk of change but staying in the old mindset" excuse has been identified. Set your mental alarm. There is no change without change.

Chapter 9

Success And Failure Are Both Scary, So It's Best To Avoid Them

Every excuse is fear-based, and will continue to rob us of the life we should be living if we allow it to.

Fear of failure is like a plague that infects the majority of the population. I know for myself there were so many things that I didn't try because of my fear of failure. I think the major issues in my mind are how I perceived failure. I used to worry that my friends and family would be disappointed in me. I would be mocked and ridiculed or I would lose the respect of the people I valued in my life, along with the people I didn't even know. I feared I would be less of a person and I would be doomed to repeat failure over and over again if I failed once. I worked it up in my mind so much that trying something new was just too dangerous a venture.

Most of our fears are based on a lack of knowledge. I finally learned that if I feared something, perhaps I should find out more about it. I started to research the fear of failure, and only then did I begin to think differently. "When you change the way you look at things, the things you look at change." – Wayne Dyer.

I started to see failure as a crucial part of growth. We are all going to fail at something in life, so why not get some kind of benefit from it? It's disappointing to fail of course, but every failure takes us one step closer to success. If I had given up on my recovery journey, I would still be horribly sick right now, or in the ground. I no longer see failure as failure; I see it as a stepping stone. I would define a complete failure as when you fail at something and then you give up completely. I embrace failure because one way or another I took action. If I fail at something, it doesn't own me! I go back to the drawing board and find another way to obtain my goal. If you are passionate enough to achieve success, you will be unstoppable!

Another excuse, that is not talked about often but has a huge impact on our decisions, is the fear of success! I have always had a major fear of success because I believed that once I succeeded, it might be too hard to deal with, and I would be obligated to repeat it. Success was such a foreign concept to me that it didn't even seem real. If I become successful, everyone will expect success from me on a regular basis. Once you succeed, others expect this of you! Expectations are hard to live up to. Success sets a very high standard, and pressures for the future. This can be a scary responsibility to live up to. We don't know what the future holds but we do know that success feels great. Why not enjoy it when you achieve it? There are no guarantees in life, but if you work hard and have the right attitude you will be more successful than not.

The "fear of failure and fear of success" excuse has been identified. Set your mental alarm. Hiding from what may or may not happen causes far more pain than going for it.

Chapter 10

What's Your Vice? – The Unspoken Excuse

We live in an addiction-based world, and everyone has one type of addiction or another. Some are socially acceptable and some are not. Our addictions play a significant role in our lives, as far as excuses go. Ask yourself, "What is my addiction?" You can try to deny it to others and yourself, but deep down you know what it is. When you finally come to terms with it, do not judge yourself; accept what it is without shame and start taking action to overcome this vice.

I can tell you that I had so many addictions that they ruled my entire existence. I had addictions to drugs, booze, cigarettes, junk food, women, gambling, and even sleep. Every waking moment my mind was fixated on one or all of my addictions. My addictions controlled my every thought and every action. These vices brought me to some very dark places, hurting everyone that I came into contact with along the way. This does not have to happen to you!

Once the addiction is identified, it is up to you to seek out the help you need. I am a firm believer that when a person is fully aware that they have an addiction but then chooses not to get some sort of aid or even attempt to overcome it on their own, they are making the conscious decision to stay in the addiction state. I knew I was sick, I knew I needed help, but I didn't care enough about myself to do anything about it. I suffered for years because I refused to make any real effort at changing. If you have a serious addiction, you are either going to overcome it, or you're going to suffer right up until you die.

Change is hard, and so it seems that pain is what is required to inspire real and genuine action. If you know right now that you have a problem, what is stopping you from getting better? Pick up a phone and take your life back. You deserve a happy and healthy life, so make this a top priority.

The "addiction" excuse has been identified. Set your mental alarm. If an addiction controls your life, reach out for help and make a decision to change.

Chapter 11

My Past Sucks And The World Owes Me

It amazes me how many people I have come across that speak about their past and how it continues to affect who they are today. It's almost like a competition to see who has had the hardest life! It's like a badge of honor to the ones who have suffered the most. They use this as a way to get out of their responsibilities and to elicit sympathy from anyone they can. They think the world owes them everything and they shouldn't have to pull their own weight. I know I did.

I certainly don't discount anyone's feelings, and I have come across people with horrific pasts. Indeed my heart goes out to them. Trying to explain to these people that, even though they have had horrible experiences, they don't have to continue on living in that mindset and ruin their future is a hard concept to sell. Coming from a life of drug addiction, I've had some pretty traumatic moments. I could have listed hundreds of stories of my pain and suffering, but that isn't the point of this book, and they are not memories I choose to allow into my thoughts anyway. It took me a long time to understand that part is all done, and it's over. If I kept thinking about myself as I was in the past, then I would be that same person in the present. If I keep bringing up my sad stories and keep going back there in my mind, I will never grow or feel happiness. When a person is always talking about how bad their life was, it can drain the energy from anyone that is around them. No one wants to be around someone who lives in that state. The poor me self-pity thing will only get you so far. Usually, self-pity leads people back to where they once were.

Dan Wischnewski

I can remember telling my tale of woe to a friend. He stopped halfway through and said, "Dan, I am so sick of you feeling sorry for yourself." He said, "You have been through some painful experiences, but I am tired of hearing them, and you are hiding behind them. It has gotten to the point I can't be around you because every time you open your mouth, you are looking for sympathy. You sound like a weak coward that hides from the present by living in the past." Wow! That stung, but he was right! There is nothing wrong with voicing pain and asking for help, but if your whole album is sad songs your future will be pretty bleak.

A common belief for people who are suffering is that they don't deserve happiness. They may have made mistakes in the past, but they are allowing these mistakes to hold them hostage. We have all made mistakes, and we have all hurt someone in our lives. This does not mean we should throw in the happiness towel. We may not be able to make up for our mistake to that particular person; I know we can't turn back the clock, but I do know we can make up for things in other ways. Help as many people as you can now, do the right thing and you will rise above and silence the voice that tells you that you are undeserving. Keep in mind you do not have to swing to the exact opposite side of the fence. I have seen all too many times people taking their past mistakes and turning themselves into a martyr. They are still playing the victim card, but now they are doing it through giving of themselves nonstop and accepting mistreatment from others to atone for their sins. This thought pattern will keep you just as sick, and your quality of life will plummet. Help others, live right, but value yourself at the same time.

The "My past sucks and the world owes me" excuse has been identified. Set your mental alarm. If you live in the past you will die in the present. It's your choice.

Chapter 12

I Am Always Tired, And I Can't See My Feet

People are tired, lack energy and are overall unhealthy. These are the same people who are making the fast food industry the successful enterprise that it is. I admit I was one of them. I didn't care enough about myself to eat healthy so my weight became a real issue. It was impossible for me to feel energetic or inspired when I was putting such unhealthy foods into my body. I was just too lazy, and I didn't care enough about myself to take the time to learn about nutrition. Cooking or preparing a meal that was good for me was way too much effort than I was willing to make. I was too tired to make an effort to eat healthy, and I stayed tired because I wasn't eating healthy foods. It's such a vicious cycle! Most people on the planet are addicted to sugar and do not even realize this. It's so much easier to go through the drive-thru than take the time to cook a healthy meal. Never mind the grocery shopping that's involved as well. The thought of eating vegetables and fruit was not something I desired or even thought of as necessary. It sure is!

We must eat healthy to have a happy life. I am not a nutritionist, but I know what is right for me and what is not. There are plenty of sources for help when it comes to nutrition and healthy eating plans that you can look into. Life is too short to feel sluggish and lazy. I knew that every day I allowed myself to eat in such an unhealthy manner, my life span was only going to grow shorter and shorter.

Dan Wischnewski

The "I'm too tired" excuse has been identified. Set your mental alarm. The second you start to think that you are too tired, your security system should identify it as an excuse and ask why. Why are you so tired? If you reflect on what you have been eating, and your level of exercise, the answer will present itself.

Chapter 13

I Have No Free Time!! I Do Have Commitments To Facebook, Twitter, Instagram And Netflix You Know!!

Have you ever noticed that the people who claim to have the busiest lives in the world will take the time to tell you all about it for an hour or two? Isn't it strange that they can talk about the Netflix marathon they just went on, but seem to have no free time ever?

I always smile when I hear someone say that they have no free time. My smile broadens when they start firing off excuse after excuse why they can't follow through with their true goals in life. I smile not because I think less of them; I smile because I played that same broken record over and over again myself. My favorite excuse stream: I work all day, I am a single dad, and then I would list off every task that I was burdened with, real or imagined. The truth is, if you want something bad enough you will make the time to get it. In most cases this means some sacrifice. I did have a busy life, but I had the option of staying up an hour later than normal or to get up an hour earlier. I could choose to cut out all the time-stealing habits that brought no real benefit to my life.

My cell phone is a curse and a blessing all wrapped up in one. I need my phone for business, but do I need it for all the social media it offers? My excuse before was I do a lot of business on social media, which is the case for many people. The only thing was how much time did I spend doing business and how much was being a voyeur?

The key is to prioritize and/or eliminate the useless distractions. I choose to stay aware of which actions are productive and which ones are not. I now place my phone in another room on silent mode because when I am working on projects it's a huge distraction. I can remember many times a project taking twice as long as it should because I would always be checking Facebook, Instagram or some other sort of social media for the latest updates.

The fact is, if you're passionate about what you want to achieve, there is always time! Going without sleep, TV or social media to reach our goals is a small price to pay for a desired life. The feeling of accomplishment far outweighs the instant gratification of our silly, distracting habits.

The "Too Busy" excuse has been identified. Set your mental alarm. When you catch yourself using this excuse ask yourself what are you so busy with? What can you do about it? Perhaps you just need to eliminate a few distractions!

Methods of Change

Here are some of the possible solutions to overcome the excuses that have been robbing you of the life you have always wanted, and deserve. You may read these and think, I have heard of these methods before. You may think to yourself that you already know all about these, because that's what I said for many years. Knowing about them and putting them into practice are two different things. I can testify to that personally. I suggest you pick out what method(s) you feel speaks to you the most. Everyone is different, so we need to use what we feel will help us the most. Starting a couple of methods may open the doors to trying more. Some of these methods will help out and kick in immediately, and some take the time to sink in but will provide you long-term benefits. Choose what is right for you, write them down and take action. These methods are what brought me from a homeless drug addict to happy, healthy, motivated and I dare say the successful person that wakes up every day, inspired and ready to create my future.

Repetition – The Foundation of my Life Program

This is the basis of every method I use. It takes time to reprogram our minds, which in turn alters our habits. I have heard it takes 30 days of constant repetition to firmly plant a new way of thinking into our mind. In my experience it takes 60 days. In other words, it may take time but the changes last a lifetime!

Starting something new can be challenging and scary. When applying the repetition principle, the fear subsides, and our confidence begins to soar. When I repeat an affirmation long enough, it becomes who I am.

It is vital to continually repeat who you wish to become and what you want to achieve. This will keep it in the forefront of your mind at all times. Repetition is what is required to form lifelong habits and to ensure that you are in the right mindset at all times.

Think it, See it, Feel it, but Most Importantly Believe it

I love this! I love this process. I take advantage of this life-altering method multiple times per day and at night. In fact, I do this whenever I get a free moment. Were you ever punished as a child for daydreaming? Yes, it is necessary to pay attention and focus on the task at hand, but when someone who was in authority told us it was wrong to do this, they committed a great disservice to our young and impressionable minds. I have read hundreds of self-help books, and this method is the most common denominator.

My advice is to daydream, use your imagination. Go off in your mind and begin to create something that you can breathe life into. This is so easy to do, and it feels amazing.

One of my personal examples is that when I set a goal to excel in a certain business, I imagine myself being called up on stage to receive an award (remember it is okay to enjoy praise and acknowledgment for a job well done). I visualize myself in a James Bond-like suit, wearing the shiniest shoes on the market, and I feel the fabric on my skin as I walk up the stairs. I imagine the bright lights all around me, and an enthused crowd consisting of my fellow business partners but most importantly my family. I see the look of pride in my parents' eyes, and I revel in the fact that they no longer have to worry whether or not their youngest son is going to make it. I see myself picking up the mic, and I feel the energy of the people in the room. I imagine speaking the words of gratitude that come from my heart, and they are spoken with reverence.

Next I adjust my focus to who I had become as a person, on my journey to the podium. How I had evolved into the person, and I can actually see myself growing! I imagine what it would feel like knowing that I worked harder than I thought possible, that I never gave up no matter what the challenges were. I become that future person in the present, if only for a little while. Knowing that I would attract all the right people and opportunities that would create this person I wanted to be. If I continued with this practice in conjunction with a plan of action of course!

Now here is the most crucial part of this ritual. You must believe it can happen. You must think in your mind it has already occurred during the time you practice this method. It is not that challenging to do once you get into it.

Meditation

When I first started meditation, I thought I had to sit cross-legged on some chair with my fingers grasped in a comical way while chanting and moaning for hours at a time. This is not the case! There are millions of different ways you can meditate that can bring peace into your life. You can gain significant benefits from meditation by just doing small intervals of this method during the day. It takes discipline to meditate if you find it hard to sit still and be quiet. Our brains, for the most part, are not disciplined and run rampant. I've heard it referred to as the "monkey mind." The monkey mind is a mind that is constantly going without any direction or any reason. An untrained mind is an unhappy mind. A mind that is not at peace. A very simple method of meditating, one that I have incorporated into my daily life, is the system of counting breaths. It's as simple as sitting on a chair with your feet firmly planted, hands on your knees, counting to ten, one - breath in, two - breathe out, etc. This is not something to grade yourself on. There is not a right way or a wrong way to do it. The best way is the way that makes you feel at peace. When unwanted thoughts jump in front of the screen on your mind that's okay. Acknowledge them and let them go.

The benefits of meditation are numerous; however, the benefits are not realized, I found, until meditation was performed consistently for a period of time. Now meditation is an ongoing practice for myself on a regular daily basis, as it calms my mind, grounds me, and then I am able to open myself up for inspirational thoughts. There are countless times where I needed an answer to a question or I had to make a serious decision and I felt at a complete loss, only to have a revelation shortly after a meditation session. I suggest that you research what type of meditation works best for you, as everyone is different. There are many outlets for meditation guidance, whether it's through a book, a video or an actual practitioner.

Nature

Connecting to nature is an amazing way to bring peace and inspiration to your life. There is a reason why most people feel a sense of euphoria when walking in the woods or walking by a water source. Do you ever notice that when you are outdoors, whether you are camping, hiking or walking on the beach, most people you come across are smiling and genuinely happy? Have you ever walked outside somewhere beautiful and took a deep breath in, and you just felt good? Human beings were not meant to be inside buildings the majority of their lives, which is why it feels so invigorating and liberating to be at one with nature. If you don't have access to nature on a daily basis, it can be just as beneficial to go for a walk to the nearest park, or as simple as sitting underneath a tree (which is an ideal place to meditate, by the way)! I have a particular spot in the heart of downtown Winnipeg by the parliament building. My special spot is a little park bench that overlooks the water and is surrounded by trees. A nice quiet, clean place to stop and relax. I try to go there on a regular basis when I need to take a pause in my life. I breathe in the fresh air and look at how beautiful the river is, so I can dial into that connection. There is nature and beauty everywhere, no matter if you live in the city or not. It's as simple as finding a spot that is convenient and accessible in your life.

Write Out Your Life Story

This is so important and can completely transform the person that you are. Of course this takes a substantial commitment and great deal of work, but I can say from personal experience how much it has improved my life. We all tell ourselves our own story within. We all base our lives on what we think we have gone through, which, by the way, takes the lead for our future thoughts. After I had written out my own story, I had such a better understanding as to who I am today. It forced me to face some pretty hard truths but it also helped me reach some memories that were holding me back. When I read my story I now find myself more willing to forgive myself, as well as others that I had held resentments towards. I was able to establish and understand my long-term patterns. I am now able to give myself credit for what I have achieved, and the obstacles that I have overcome. Focusing on who I was, was painful but also an act of freedom. I was finally able to let the same old negative thinking patterns go and begin to replace them with thoughts that make me feel good about the person I am today. Writing out my story allowed me to bring closure to my past, and gave me the ability to create my future unencumbered.

Start Teaching

When I was struggling with my depression and anxiety along with my addiction, I actually started teaching others how to live a happy and healthy life. I felt like a complete hypocrite at the time but it was exactly what I needed. How I started was by giving a speech called "The Keys to Happiness." I went from function to function with my powerpoint presentation. I had all the solutions listed out, and the strategies on how anyone can incorporate them into their lives. Teaching others made me feel amazing! I felt like I was making a difference. Just as importantly, I knew I had to live the way I was teaching so I took this to heart. The more I taught, the more I studied. The more questions I was asked, the more inspired I became to learn the answers. Having someone say that what I had to offer helped them live a better life made all that hard work and time worthwhile. This is one of those situations where I had to fake it until I made it. The only difference is I was held accountable for someone else besides myself.

Affirmations

Everyone has heard of affirmations. They have been spoken of and taught to people for many years. They are an excellent way of shaping your mind and staying on point. Doing affirmations can be a simple concept to follow, and all that is required is to write out the traits and thinking patterns that you wish to have as your own. I've used affirmations for years, and it has made a world of difference. I have a very strict regimen that has now become ingrained in my routine. Right before I go to bed I read my affirmation list. I want these key and critical thoughts implanted into my mind before I fall asleep. I want my last thoughts before going into a dream state to be the ones that I have selected. Upon waking the first thing I do is roll over and grab my affirmation list and read it. This puts the ideals right into the forefront of my mind.

I strongly suggest you make a short list at first – ten affirmations maximum. There was a time when I had ten pages. It became a chore to read and lost all meaning. The most efficient way is to write out a list of things that are the most important to you, what you want most in life. These affirmations will jump off the page at you. They will make you feel a sense of excitement and desire as you read them. You will start to actually feel them! An affirmation list is an always changing thing. Eventually you become what you are affirming, and then once that happens it is time to change your list. You want constant growth. The affirmations that become less important in time probably were not what you really in your heart wanted to do. I let go of certain affirmations on my list when I no longer feel passionate about them. Once I let them go I replace them with new ones! You are always evolving on your path, so it is important to follow your heart and instincts. That is our natural guidance system.

Incantations

This is a method rarely discussed and rarely used by most. I like to think of it as another form of affirmations, just a much more aggressive style. Incantations choosing a particular power phrase that is shouted out loud and with absolute emotion. This method inspires you and commands your full attention. It will get your heart pumping! Most people find this embarrassing and uncomfortable, but there are ways of doing it to alleviate these fears. My personal method is when I am in my car, driving down the highway, I will scream at the top of my lungs "I AM UNSTOPPABLE" (I stole that from Tony Robbins). Others that I like to shout at the top of my lungs are, "I AM DESTINED FOR SUCCESS!" or "I WILL HELP OTHERS!"

Keep in mind while I am screaming this in my car like a lunatic, I am laughing; it is fun! It's an incredible stress reliever and it makes you feel powerful and in a ready state for action. This is an excellent way to get pumped up for an activity.

Volunteer

If you want to get out of your own head, help others. Find a cause that has a deep meaning to you and jump right in. There are so many benefits to being a volunteer. For me, it takes my personal stress away. When helping others, I no longer focus on my own wants. I find it pretty hard to be depressed or anxious when I am helping others.

Being a volunteer for the United Way has given me real purpose; it is something I believe in. When my actions or words help someone to live a better life, I live a better life. I have made real, genuine lifelong friends, both in the people I am helping and the people I work with within this organization.

Look at the health benefits to being a volunteer: you stay active, and socializing is good for the body and soul.

Volunteering also has an impact on your resumé or chosen career. Many business opportunities have come from my volunteer work. People see through your actions that you are a caring person who has an interest in helping others. This is a sought-after trait by potential employers or business partners.

If everyone set aside time to do volunteer work on a regular basis, the whole world would be a better place. I firmly believe that people are genuinely good, and if they are ever given a chance they will help anyone they can.

If you feel as if you do not have time to get involved with an organized volunteer program that's okay. You can reap many of the same benefits by acts of kindness. I commit to acts of kindness as often as I can. In the past, I did them so I would receive praise. In time I outgrew that need and automatically do them because of the feeling it gives me. Helping others makes me feel necessary and a part of the solution. An act of kindness can have a life-changing effect on a person.

I had a relative stranger stop and gave me encouragement and advice on an upcoming event I was involved in. This exchange only took a few moments but helped me when I needed it. That person didn't realize how important their words were to me and my future. I believe that people come in and out of our lives for a reason. When your mindset is to help, then you can better understand why they came into your life.

YouTube to Shift Your Energy

I love YouTube; it helped me to shift from one mindset to another when I desperately needed it. There are many other sources online, and I have no financial gain by recommending YouTube. It is my preferred source. This is my go-to when I am having trouble shifting out of a nasty mood or funk. If I am feeling down and can't seem to shake it off, I will search on YouTube's wide selection of Acts of Kindness. It will amaze you how quickly your mood will shift. Viewing acts of kindness reaffirms that the world is good, and so are most of the people in it. Watching someone put their needs aside to help someone else's lifts my spirits and inspires me to take the same action. I quickly forget what issue I am dwelling on, and this puts my mind into a better perspective. I can go from a dark mood to one of happiness and the willingness to help others in a matter of minutes.

I also go to YouTube for motivation. I search motivational speakers, crank it up, and go after my workout of the day. These speeches are usually accompanied by inspirational music that raises my energy level. I can go from feeling lethargic to explosive power in a matter of moments. Not only does this increase my energy; it also teaches me something new about myself. It plants lasting seeds. Listening to a form of motivation is an absolute must; it is something I do on a daily basis. I find myself thinking of certain quotes that have been hammered into my mind over time. It seems whenever a negative thought rears its energy-draining head, a positive quote pops in my mind to counter it. I can't recommend it enough to use this as a daily ritual.

The Bus, Train, and Your Car are Your Classroom

A majority of people spend their commute to work listening to talk radio or music. This is fine at times, but think of the benefits of using that time to learn something new. Just imagine how much you could learn, and how much growth could take place on a daily basis. Envision what you could accomplish in a full year of doing this consistently. That hour a day can add up fast, and so can the knowledge you absorb. I have heard of people who have learned a new language by listening to programs just going to and from work. My focus has been spiritual growth. I listen to a wide variety of spiritualists on a daily basis. It is pretty hard to allow negative thoughts inside your mind when you are always surrounded by positive reinforcements. Nowadays most use podcasts as a source of program. I am old school. I go to the library and check out CDs. I pick out whatever course jumps out at me, listen to it a couple of times, then I return and replace.

Surround Yourself with the Right People

You are what and who you surround yourself with. Start making the cuts. The simplest way is to gauge your energy level. When you speak to or are around a certain person, and your energy level consistently goes down, cut them out. If it is someone who has been in your life for an extended period of time, you need to have the conversation with them. Let them know how you feel, and you could possibly even be doing them a favor. Taking this action will reveal your real relationship. I have had some people take it to heart and change the way they conduct themselves, and thank me for having the courage to say something. I have also had people tell me to go to hell, which reaffirmed they were not someone I wanted in my life anyway.

Surround yourself with like-minded people. If you want to be a success in life, spend your time around successful people. It is incredible how being around people with purpose and goals in life can elevate you to a higher level. It's equally amazing how quickly you can be dragged down by people who have zero interest in living their best life. Those are the dream-killers. When you speak of your goals, and they find fault in them and dissuade you from pursuing them, it's because they feel threatened. They are scared you will outgrow them. Your success forces them to look at where they are. It's easier to find fault and cast doubt then to admit they need to change themselves.

I have heard that looking at the five people you spend the most time with will tell you exactly who you are, where you are in life and in which direction you are headed.

It only takes one bad apple to spoil the bunch. In the past, I was that bad apple that you were warned of. I have seen the effects one misguided person with a negative attitude can have on an entire group. Get rid of any of the energy-drainers in your life, and you will be doing yourself a long-term favor.

Forgiveness

We have all seen posts on Facebook or other social media on how important it is to forgive. I suspect as most people scroll by such posts. They might possibly give it a like, but do they ever give it any real thought? If you were to take a moment right now and think of how many people you have resentment towards, how many would there be? When you envision the person or situation, how does it make you feel? How many hours out of your life have you obsessed on some former hurt or insult? How many sleepless nights have you had to relive a certain scenario? I think most of us have heard the saying "forgiving someone is setting you free." How many of us take it to heart?

I can remember having such hatred for certain people or events. I can remember letting it take over the majority of my thoughts. I would even add to the resentment by creating a situation in my mind far worse than what it really was. I can constantly remember daydreaming of revenge, and outright plotting at night. My anger was so intense that it made me physically sick. I was told in a recovery program that if you want to forgive someone, pray for them. That you should wish genuinely for great things to happen for them. This may be a useful method for some, but it wasn't for me. I would start "praying" for them; it would start off nice then turn into a malevolent prayer, with me praying for their painful and untimely demise. Wishing someone else pain is only putting out negative energy, which will come back to you, not them.

I found the way to let go was to care enough for myself to let it go. I would reason with the other voices in my head that these thoughts were hurting me and not helping me. I would also remind myself that every time I thought this way, that person or event owned me. I am not fond of the idea of being held by anything, so I was able to forgive, not for them but for me. I cherish my happiness. It doesn't matter if I was completely innocent in a situation and was wronged. The fact is, would I rather rot from the inside out and allow the person or situation to further damage my life? The answer is no.

Just as important as forgiving others is forgiving ourselves. I have hurt and let down many people in my life. Forgiving myself was not an easy thing to do. The realization came to me that feeling bad about myself all the time benefits no one. You need to give yourself a break and feel some self-compassion. Forgiveness truly is freedom.

Celebrate Victories Big and Small

It is so important to celebrate your steps towards progress. In the past I would achieve a certain goal, and instead of celebrating it I would condemn myself for taking too long or not executing it better. We are taught as kids to not brag or be arrogant, but that advice should have been in two parts. Yes, we shouldn't be conceited, but we should be encouraged to be proud of ourselves. Telling a friend or a family member of an accomplishment is not bragging, it's sharing your life with them. If you are sharing this information with the right people, they will encourage you. There is also a good chance that they will become inspired to go after something they have always wanted to do. I had an old friend contact me when he saw I was releasing my book. He said he had always dreamed of writing a book, and if someone like me could do it then there is no reason he couldn't. Not the kind of praise I would prefer, but if it helped him out then so be it. Make sure you celebrate the small stuff. Any step forward is a victory. If I learn something new that is worth celebrating. I reward myself with something simple, which makes it all worthwhile and helps keep me on the path. When I achieve a significant goal, I make a tremendous deal out of it. In the past, I have rewarded myself with as little as a fancy dinner right up to taking a trip somewhere tropical. Celebrating forces you to appreciate what you have done. It is such a wonderful feeling, that becomes a lifelong cherished memory. It makes all that hard work and perseverance worthwhile. It also is something that you will want to experience over and over again. When I have one of these moments I focus more on the person I have become rather than the actual achievement. This is where the joy of my personal evolution comes in.

Inner Talk

Making a conscious effort to be aware of all your inner thoughts is a necessity. We have a multitude of voices yapping in our ears. It is up to us to decide what we will allow and what we won't. This takes time and practice, but it will be ultimately what dictates your happiness and future. We must constantly filter our thoughts. It's a simple evaluation; does this thought hurt me or help me? Does this thought bring happiness or pain into my life? Does this idea cause me to worry and stress? If it does cause harm, it must be acknowledged, then countered and let go.

What happens if the voice in your head keeps repeating the same thing over and over again? How do you get rid of it? The answer is getting really pissed off!! Remember that you run the show, you control your thoughts, and any unwanted thoughts are countered and dispatched instantly.

The second my inner voice tells me that I am tired, my immediate response is "I am energy!!" Many times while exercising a voice will start whining "This is too hard, it's okay to stop now." My voice of power booms "I will finish." When the voice starts to make me doubt my future goals, my voice of power resonates "I Am Successful; I create my future!!" When the voice finds fault in others, my voice of power echoes "I am someone that helps, not hurts!"

The important thing here is to counter whatever disempowering thoughts you are having, to rationalize how you want to think and feel. Focus on what you want, never on what you don't want. The more you concentrate on the positive things, the stronger these become, and in turn the negative fear voices will weaken.

Exercise & Diet

There is no way of getting around this; exercise and diet are crucial. I have struggled with my weight on and off for years. I developed what I consider an eating disorder due to my past drug addiction. When I was in the sickness, I would drop drastic amounts of weight and be unable to stomach food. When I was in a clean state I would binge eat because it was almost like a self-defense mechanism. I would shovel food down by the troughful, because I was always worried it would be a long time before I would be able to eat again. During long periods of clean time, I would put on a massive amount of weight. It is certainly not healthy to go up and down all the time. At some points in my life I would be in fantastic shape, and at other times my stomach would rest on the steering wheel. What I can tell you without reservation is being overweight does not feel right. It genuinely messed with my mind. I did not feel attractive, but more importantly, my health suffered. At my worst points, I would feel lethargic, depressed, and disappointed in myself.

Like most, I was well aware that I should be eating better quality foods but I wasn't big on the taste, and I was way too lazy to cook something with nutritional merit. I had to make a decision to care about myself. I found changing my habits in small increments was the way to go. I had jumped into crazy diet fads before, but realistically they were not long term. If you feed me a chicken breast and broccoli every day I will become a starving, unhappy lunatic. The way that I was able to make better food choices was by setting a mental alarm every time I ate. It's simple. When I am about to put whatever food into my mouth, I ask myself "Is this going to help my body or hurt it?" It only took a short while for this to become a habit. There have been many times when asking myself this question when I have yelled "Yes! This pizza and chocolate are not good for me, but I don't give a sh*t! right now so go to hell, food voice!"

I am a firm believer that we should enjoy our time on the planet, so I encourage having treats once in a while. I was and I am still involved in a special weight-loss product that I started using; it helped make the whole process so much easier. This product is simple to use and good for my body, so I welcomed it with open arms. If you would like info on what I am doing, send an email to bigdreamsbiggerexcuses@gmail.com.

Get a gym membership and spend a minimum of 3 hours a day pumping iron!! Nope, I do not recommend this unless you are passionate about training. Pick something you genuinely like to do that is active, and do it on a regular basis. It can be a simple process, but most overcomplicate it. We all know that our bodies need exercise to be healthy and feel good, but why do so few follow through?

When I was overweight, I hated to exercise. There were times when staggering on the treadmill that I considered wearing a sports bra (a Bro or Manziere).

I tried to lift and train at the same level I did when I was in shape. Big mistake. I would be so sore that I couldn't move for days, and would usually pick up an injury of some kind. I would associate the pain with the act of exercise, and not my ridiculous mindset. I would then secure my place back in the ass groove of my lazy boy chair.

Exercise can be anything that has you active and moving. I have found the biggest mistake people make is trying to get in shape in a way they don't enjoy. Keep it simple. No matter what you do, be active every single day of your life. We were not designed to sit at a desk all day, only to transition onto the couch. The hard part can be to get started; I can certainly agree with that. I suggest you have a friend or family member join you. As a team you can help motivate each other and enjoy each other's company at the same time! What may have started as a dreaded task has now become a fun event. Have a good time with it, and laugh and be silly. Most of us are not training for the Olympics, so do the work but enjoy doing it. Use your shield against the crybaby, lazy voice. When it starts chirping, counter it. If it says "I am tired" you counter with "I am energy!" If it says "Stop," you yell "I Am Power!!"

Imagine how it would feel to be in the shape and feel the health benefits that you have always wanted. Keep this constantly in your mind while you train. This will keep you inspired and motivated. The cool thing about exercise is it becomes addictive. A healthy addiction as I see it. I exercise every day; my body has become accustomed to this pattern. If I ever miss a day, I feel very off and anxious. I need that stress relief and healthy high I get when working out. I think everyone does. Life is so much more enjoyable when feeling confident, powerful, energetic and healthy.

This combination of a strengthened mind and momentum will ensure your long-term success.

Goal Setting and Time Management

To get anywhere in life, goals and time management are a must. I have an old-school daytimer that I use every day. Wherever I go, it comes along with me. It is important to write down your ultimate goal, then break it down into smaller goals that will lead you to this final goal. I have been told many times to be realistic with my goals and the time in which I will realize them. I agree and disagree with this piece of advice. I believe it is important to have whatever goal feels right to you. Do not allow someone else's limited imagination downsize something that you in your heart believe is possible. Many of the goals I have achieved were done in direct conflict with another's opinion of what is realistic or not. The timeframe should be what you feel is achievable. I make sure to have an end date for what I am trying to achieve. As I conquer the smaller goals on my quest, I can better gauge a realistic timeframe for the overall completion. I do not allow the word realistic to become an excuse to coast and extend the deadline. I know in my gut if I have been putting in the proper work amount or not. I know if I have been utilizing my time efficiently and if I shut the door to any distractions because I review my day every night before bed.

Sunday night is my planned strategy time, when I write out my daily goals for the upcoming week. I always know what I have to do, and when I will be doing it, well in advance. My system does drive many of my loved ones nuts but is a critical tool for me. I refuse to wing it as

I waste so much time and effort figuring out what to do next if there isn't a plan in place.

When I review my large and lead-up goals on a daily basis, I feel a sense of purpose, motivation and excitement as I draw close to completion.

Thank you

That whole gratitude thing is always thrown around and, to be honest, would irritate my senses as it was a word that was thrust upon me on a regular basis. I had so many preachy people remind me of how I should be grateful I am still alive, and that I am where I am. I might have agreed internally, but I resented it being put in my face on a regular basis. It took a long time for it to sink in as to how powerful gratitude is. Sometimes if you believe in an idea but you don't like how it's labeled, it is beneficial to rename it in a way that feels right to you. Therefore I rarely use the word gratitude; I speak about the power of Thank You. I may be splitting hairs, but it is what works for me.

The power of saying thank you raises my energy and helps me get through any and all challenges that come my way. All I have to do is remember how it was and how it is now, and very few challenges can compare. The Power of Thanks has strengthened my relationships with everyone in my life. Showing appreciation to my family, that has stood by me no matter what, is not only important to me but to them as well. People may or may not say it openly, but I suspect everyone likes to hear a kind word of appreciation. I find that I sleep so much better when I am thankful for everything in my life. It provides me with a warm glow of security.

Say thank you every day, and think of all the things you are thankful for on a regular basis, and you will find a new sense of peace that you didn't have before.

Do What Makes You Happy

What is the point of living if you aren't enjoying your life? We are all going to die; that's a fact. Why rob yourself of a happy existence? Life is busy, and everyone has responsibilities, but you have a responsibility to be happy as well. When a person lives their life to just get by, they are barely existing. I see people who are so inundated with tasks that their lives are passing them by. If you want to be a great parent, partner or employee, you must have a source of fun in your life. If you do the things that make you happy, you are a happier person! This is a pretty straightforward concept. This benefits everyone that you come into contact with. I know when I have my Dan time to do the things I enjoy, I am a better person overall. You should never feel guilty for wanting something for yourself. It is mandatory.

Review Day

When you review your day every night before your bedtime, it will allow you to see what direction you're going in. A simple moment of reflection can bring you such enlightenment. This will establish what your "triggers" are for certain behaviors. It is important to remember how you felt during the day when doing certain tasks.

There was a time in my life when around 2:00 pm I stopped working hard, my attitude stunk and I was easily frustrated. I could not understand why this was until I broke down my day and how I felt during it. I realized I was eating a very early lunch! I know this may sound silly, but for me an empty stomach can be a ticking time bomb. I have to keep my blood sugars at a certain level or I become a loose cannon. A very simple tweak was to eat lunch just a little later and have snacks readily available. I had to also incorporate an alarm system on my phone, so I would remember to eat. If I am engaged in my work, time can fly by and I don't realize that I haven't eaten for hours.

I not only track my performance, but I ask myself how I treated others and what my motivation was. If my motivation was self-serving or purely money based, then I know I'm heading down the wrong path and correct it immediately. I am a firm believer that if you help others get what they need in life, you will get what you need.

I am okay with making mistakes, but it always feels better if I can right any wrongs I have committed, willingly or not.

When I identify an error that needs correcting, I write it down and set a plan of action to take care of it. I do not dwell on my mistakes; I correct them the best I can and move on.

Daily reflection helps identify any and all negative patterns, which could allow for a solution. Without thought, the negative trends will not only continue but will grow into a strong habit. Why allow something to fester and become a real issue that will take lots of your time and effort to combat?

That being said, reflection is usually a very positive time to give yourself a pat on the back! In the spirit of celebrating victories big and small, I allow myself to feel proud of what I have accomplished on any particular day.

Accept Help

I used to think that taking help from other people was a sign of weakness. That could not have been further from the truth. It takes lots of courage to reach out for help when it's needed. When you accept help you are forming a bond of trust with the person you are asking. The majority of individuals on the planet are more than willing to lend a hand. You are actually helping that person from whom you are asking help (if that makes any sense). I know for myself that it feels fantastic when someone asks for my help. It makes me feel needed and respected.

If asking for help will significantly improve your life, then ask; you deserve it. You will get your chance to help someone else down the line if you're concerned with the Karma thing; it will all balance out. I can tell you that I had quite a few people come into my life and help me when I needed it most. I am now in the position to give back, and this is something I take very seriously.

Leave Notes

Write little notes of encouragement to yourself and leave them around all the time. I open my daytimer, and boom, there is a note to me saying "Think of how your life will change if you take this particular action today." I also place notes on my elliptical saying "Work hard, lazy ass" (this always makes me laugh; there are no limits to my coveted geekdomness). I will leave a note in my car saying "Be thankful for the wheels because it's only your mode of transportation, not a home." These are examples of what I do for myself, and this act adds encouragement and laughter when I need it. I also like to use my little note game to make others smile. I put a note in my girlfriend's car saying how much I love her. Imagine waking up and going to work, and finding a note of love taped to the steering wheel. I leave notes for my son in his lunch bag, telling him how proud I am of him. The power of leaving notes can improve your life and everyone else's around you. It is fast and easy to do but can make a difference in someone's life, so why not incorporate it into your life?

Seek out a Mentor

I have a number of mentors currently in my life. Learning from someone who has already gone down the same road you're traveling can save you years of frustration. In the past, I refused to accept anyone's guidance or advice because I thought I had all the answers. If that were true I wouldn't have lived my life the way that I did. The Personal Coaching business has exploded over the years, and rightfully so. When you have a mentor or a life coach that will educate and motivate you, it can make a drastic difference in your progress and your quality of life.

Keep Your Promises and Be Honest

We are only as good as our word. This is what defines who we are, and the life we are going to live. In my addiction, I was a pathological liar. I lied so often it became second nature. I made promises to everyone and would break them mere minutes after declaring them. It is a pretty awful feeling when everyone in your life refuses to take you seriously and has zero faith in you.

If you were to look through my daytimers for the last 15 years, you would see goals and events and activities that I promised I would take part in, where I never followed through. The pattern was set, and it became part of who I was. Every time I broke a promise to myself, my self-esteem and my self-worth lowered. It's impossible to respect yourself when you can so easily let yourself and others around you down.

After I came out of the fog and developed a conscience, I made it my mission to be honest, and keep my promises. I heard Judge Judy say "When you tell the truth you don't need a good memory." I sure wish that I had heard her say that years ago; it would have made my life so much easier. It did take a lot of effort, commitment and memory to juggle all the many lies I used to tell. It was exhausting and kept me constantly on guard. I could never remember what I said to all the different people that came in and out of my life. I was caught in lies on a regular basis. I would go into cover-up mode and make it worse with additional lies.

The relief I felt telling the truth, whether it was good or bad, was liberating. My stress levels went down and my self-confidence started to rise. A positive voice in my head would say "You see, it's not that hard to be honest, and look how great it makes you feel." We all know when we are about to tell a lie. Before you follow through ask yourself is it necessary? Do I have to be a liar to make myself feel better or to get one over on someone? Isn't it easier to tell the truth and avoid all the long-time suffering that will follow you throughout your life? Good or bad, tell the truth and live free.

Keeping our promises to others is what shows them they are a priority, and have great value in our lives. When we keep our promises, we earn respect, trust and karma points. Keeping our promises opens up doors for opportunity and future rewards. I can't stress enough how important it is to keep your promises to yourself. When you break a promise to yourself, it says you don't care enough to value your life.
Do not allow promise breakers in your life. Slip-ups happen; forgiveness and a second chance is a reasonable route to take, but when a person regularly breaks their promises to you, it's time to make some cuts. We have no room in our lives for liars and promise breakers. They hurt our feelings and disappoint us time and time again. If they do not care enough about you to respect you with the essential traits of truth and honesty, then they must be bounced from your life. Quality people only allowed.

My Personal Ritual

Morning – The second my alarm goes off I jump out of bed. I have learned over the years that even with a good night's sleep if I press snooze, even once, I feel drained when I get up. I make sure that my alarm is one that is peaceful. Waking up to a bomb shelter alarm will inspire rage, not peace.

I roll over and reach for my affirmation list and read it over. We have a packed house with family up and about at different times, so I will make sure to get up before everyone else so I can read it in the peace and quiet. Getting up early to set the pace for the day is a small sacrifice to make.

Reading my affirmations reignites the desire of who I am becoming and what I wish to achieve. This immediate focus inspires and motivates me. While I am reading my affirmation list, I take my time and visualize the goal and feel like it has already happened. This is a form of meditation; it raises my energy level and puts a smile on my face. I then review my goals for the day in my old-school daytimer. I know what needs to be done and what time I need to do it.

Throughout the day I make sure that I am eating healthy foods and drinking plenty of water. The food I put in my body and the frequency that I eat has a dramatic effect on my energy levels as well as my mood. I can get pretty crazy and irrational if I have an empty stomach. Next, I exercise. I only train for 30- 60 minutes, but I make sure I do it daily. While I am exercising, I listen to a form of motivation and again visualize and feel myself living the life I want. It's quite a rush when I see and feel in my head what it would be like to accomplish a certain goal. If you believe in the Law of Attraction, this is the foundation.

Next, I take action, and it is crucial for me to eliminate all distractions. I used to lose countless hours of my day on social media or texting. When it's dedicated work time, it's time to work. I have my daytimer open so I know exactly what needs to be accomplished, and then I begin. My first task is usually the one that seems the least appealing. I get the most challenging tasks done right away. This gives me a sense of pride and makes the latter tasks that much more enjoyable.

When I am stumped, looking for an answer or just need calm down, I sneak in 10 minutes of meditation. It amazes me how the answer of inspiration comes to me in a short period right after meditating.

I make sure that I have scheduled happy breaks. I like to stop and go for a walk, meditate or do something else fun. This is like a form of mini celebration. I worked hard, so I reward myself. It gives me an extra experience to look forward to. This has a profound effect on my sustained happiness.

I am a self-proclaimed nerd, for which I take great pride. I mention this because I write myself little notes to refer to. Things like "You're almost there; keep pushing" or "Imagine what it is going to feel like when you accomplish this……" No, I do not look in the mirror and tell myself how people like me and I am great like a *Saturday Night Live* skit.

I make sure to monitor my self-talk at all times. In the past, it was very easy to find fault in myself or anything else in my life. When one of the voices even dares suggest a complaint or a worry I instantly shift into Thank you mode. I think of where I was, where I am now, and my family. I also show that particular voice who is the boss by shifting to the thoughts that bring happiness. No disempowering thoughts allowed. I have to stay vigilant with this because in the past I could take a slight problem and create an end-of-the-world situation in my mind.

This mindset is like a shield to any negative people I may encounter as well. I call it my spiritual protection; all the negative vibes from others just bounce right off me. I refuse to be dragged down by a person choosing to live in misery.

I spend lots of time driving in my car because I live outside of the city. While I am driving, I am learning. On average I spend 2-3 hours a day in the car, so I make the best of it by listening to some course that will teach me something goal-oriented or spiritually based. Learning new things is a necessity for my growth. It makes a world of difference in my life.

I make sure to help anyone and everyone that I come in contact with. Holding a door, saying something nice and offering to help in any way that I can.

When I am finished my work day, I spend real quality time with my family. I have huge goals in life, but I found in the past, what good are your goals if you put all the people you love on the side? Finding a balance is a must. I set aside blocks of time in my daytimer to give my family my undivided attention. I am also a firm believer in going the extra mile towards my dreams, so working at night after my son is asleep is a common occurrence.

My night-time ritual is one of planning, peace and reflection.

Every night before bed I think of how I spent my day. I ask myself simple questions like "Am I proud of who I was today? Did I take actions that have brought me steps closer to my goals? Did I learn something that will make me a better person inside? Did I help other people along the way? Did I keep my promises to others and myself?" When the answer is no, I don't beat myself up; I figure out why I acted the way I did and make a point not to repeat the same mistakes.

When the answer is yes, I congratulate myself and smile.

I make sure to review what my goals are for the week, but more importantly what the plan is for tomorrow.

The last step, which is incredibly important, is to read over my affirmations. I want the last thoughts before I go into a dream state to be the ones I have chosen and believe in.

Congratulations!

You made it to the end. The excuses have been identified and exposed for what they are. You now have a multitude of methods that can aid you in your quest. The question is, will you use them? Will you pick up a pen and write down what methods would suit you best? Will you take action towards the life you have dreamed of and deserve?

Don't look back years from now with regret; start now.

Imagine what your life could be like if you were living excuse-free!

Life is good!

www.ingramcontent.com/pod-product-compliance
Lightning Source LLC
LaVergne TN
LVHW020936090426
835512LV00020B/3388